Discerning
the
Times

Discerning
the
Times

THE CHURCH IN TODAY'S WORLD

PHILIP MAURY

NIKOS A. NISSIOTIS

P.A. LIÉGÉ

Translated by Sister Agnes Cunningham, SSCM

Divine Word Publications
TECHNY, ILLINOIS

NIHIL OBSTAT
Charles Heris, OP

IMPRIMI POTEST
J. Koff, OP

IMPRIMATUR
J. Hottot, VG
Paris, April 30, 1966

(The *nihil obstat, imprimi potest,* and *imprimatur* for this
book apply only to "Church of the World," by P. A. Liégé, OP.)

Divine Word Publications is an apostolate of the Society of
the Divine Word serving the people of God throughout the
world by spreading the word.

Library of Congress Catalog Card Number: 68-8361

Printed in the United States of America

Contents

PART THREE • P.A. LIEGE

Church of the World

Foreword

The words "Church" and "world" set side by side define in one stroke one of the major problems presented to the Churches today. How can Christian societies escape the profound mutations which affect all human societies?

It is a commonplace to say that we find ourselves in a "post-Christian" age and to proclaim the end of the "Constantinian era." Such expressions are meaningless, since the traits of our civilization are no longer determined in reference to ancient Christianity. The great classic ideologies, by which the bastard offspring of Christianity were formerly denounced, are already in a state of decline. The family is a fading image. Neither the "Christian world" nor its adversaries weigh very heavily on the choices of this world. The new secularism does not embrace the heritage of former cultural patterns. Its attention is fixed on the single law of development for the ceaseless perfectioning of the instrument of its own technique, determining of itself the limits of human potentialities. Its domain lies where transcendence no longer exists and where the question of meaning has become pointless.

Christians find themselves badly prepared for this evolution which seems to challenge their traditional teachings and to mock their prophecies. They stand with divided interests between the desire to gather into isolated communities and the determination to lose themselves through sharing in common and universal aspirations. Memories of their past history, isolated from the total tradition of the Church, offer them enough reasons to bring their thoughts and attitudes into conformity with their fears as well as with their hopes.

But is it really necessary to choose between flight from the world and flight from the Church? Who can say with certainty today which way leads out of Egypt in a return from exile toward an encounter with the Lord who comes to us in time? The Churches have set to work toward an agreement between their doctrine and their manner of living in the world. They have done so with courage, in a task which they still perform awkwardly though they perceive its value. In 1965 Vatican II adopted its Pastoral Constitution on the Church in the Modern World. In 1966 the Ecumenical Council of Churches held its world conference on "The Church and Society." A dialogue of sometimes ferocious intensity has been initiated between laity and clergy, between young and old, between "movements" and "hierarchies," between "left" and "right." New loyalties can be discerned, no longer consonant with the old ecclesiastical and theological frontiers.

This new attempt to establish contact with contemporary reality is not painless. Many among us are disturbed. This concern can help us to appreciate the importance of the enterprise. We are asked to reevaluate the vocation, the mission, and thus the existence of the people of God in an entirely new situation. We are asked to free the tradition of the Gospel from those historical accretions which weigh it down and paralyze it. We are asked above all to learn, as it were, for the first time the meaning of the earliest affirmations of faith, with their ultimate consequences for a world which, in being what it is, is precisely that which "God has so loved as to give his only Son."

This exploration of the true relation of the Church and the world is imposed simultaneously on all Christian communities and confessions. It designates a special ecumenical terrain where dialogue between Churches is immediately possible.

The word "dialogue" is used deliberately. It is not yet time for an understanding which, today, would have no more meaning than a diplomatic formality. Christian unanimity today would do little more than smooth over the enormous compromises which in one way or another bind the individual Churches to some extent, encouraging their latent Manicheanism. As an evangelical heritage of primitive polemic, controversy can place at the service of Christian unity the resources of reproof, entreaty, and exhortation (2 Tim. 4:2) which built the apostolic Church. Dialogue also enables each Church to hear the word of God from the mouths of others, not only from its own preaching.

This book is meant to do more than seek out the ways of common approach to the questions asked. The authors (two of whom are laymen) start with the traditions of their own Churches to initiate a conversation in which the thought presented by each one is attended to sympathetically, sometimes objected to, and always stimulated toward a goal which brethren who are still "separated" can reach only together.

All three of these men are witnesses to a theological renewal which for several decades now has rediscovered in the sovereignty of the Lord Jesus Christ one of the most fruitful motives of ecumenical thought and action. In this ancient confession of faith they help us to perceive the immense question which is asked of Christians today: What is the significance of the belief that Jesus Christ is Lord of the Church and of the world?

M. Ferrier-Welti

PART ONE

In the Service of the World

PHILIP MAURY

CHURCH AND WORLD
IN CRISIS

THE PRESENT crisis of civilization is commonly
acknowledged. Here, the Western world is in crisis because of an increasingly acute consciousness of its growing weakness and its uncertainty about the future. There,
the Communist world hesitates between a mechanistic,
impersonal orthodoxy and the humanistic liberation of
recent years. Again, the crisis touches upon the potential
future of the Third World, once the years of inevitable
instability have been undergone. On every side, it seems
that history has gone mad or, perhaps more precisely,
that it can no longer be reduced to a rational order.

Even thirty years ago, the future of mankind seemed
clear. It was virtually determined by cultural and scientific situations. Today, anything and everything seem
possible. No solution is a priori excluded from any
problem, because present-day orientations are too in-
definite, too imprecise, too diversified. There are, it is
true, some indications of simplification. For example,
there is a growing convergence of socialistic and capi-

talistic systems toward a single universe in a collectivity of production and abundance. This convergence, however, still comes as an unexpected, embarrassing shock to contemporary intellectual systems. Besides, there is an increasing complexity in the elements of our civilization, with their apparent contradictions and the consequent unpredictability of their evolution. Today, the future of Southeast Asia without a doubt rests as much on electronic and psychological techniques and on Western collectivist totalitarian organization as on the ancient religions whose common denominator is negation of the visible, material world and nostalgia for nothingness or a pantheism as far removed as possible from Western conceptions.

In the same way, there is a simultaneous development in Western Europe and North America of conflicting values. On one hand, the materialism of a philosophy of abundance and the fermentation of new ideas and values have been born together on the ruins of rationalistic scientism. This latter, on the other hand, has been destroyed by the intrinsic developments of contemporary science and its relativism, by the aesthetic revolt of surrealistic and abstract art, and by existential philosophy in all its forms. The political and social crisis of our world cannot be understood if we do not first of all become aware of the internal disintegration of all those systems which conflicted with one another up until the middle of our century, though without ambiguity, because each of them possessed its own structure and its clear, certain value.

In order to understand the present crisis, it is necessary to take into account ideological, philosophical, and religious factors. Even more, however, attention must be given to the material and physical transformations of our universe, for these underlie the intellectual crisis.

Thus, modern collectivism has no meaning except against the background of the demographic explosion. The political philosophy of abundance reflects in a positive way the unification of the terrestrial globe in one common market, providing and consuming with assurance the inexhaustible flow of natural resources. At the same time, it is a negative reminder of the overwhelming panic of men in the face of the hunger experienced by two-thirds of mankind. Aesthetic revolutions proceed from the discovery of the infinite complexity of nature, but also from man's confrontation with his own mental and psychic complexity. They come, too, from the fluidity of thought which has been deprived of any unshakeable point of reference through physical relativism.

In a word, our era suffers from every kind of uncertainty. This extends from the liquidation of the most firmly established values and traditions to the malaise of men who are aware of their inability to understand, that is, to grasp and control the universe around them. This is the case even at a moment when science and technology promise ever more effective domination of the world. This domination may be one of both production and action: destructive action reaching a scale never before attained and creative action, perhaps at the most mysterious of all levels, that of life itself.

Thus our days are composed of contradictions. Man knows more and more only to perceive more clearly the temporary, limited character of his knowledge. His action upon nature is ever more efficacious but he remains incapable of assuring the survival of the species or his own self-domination. On the eve of mastering the world, he comes face to face with his own slavery and ignorance. Even as he brings to perfection all means of communication, he recognizes his own isolation from others. As he is borne along on multiple waves of information, the omnipresence of the "now" seems to prevent him from realizing either knowledge of the future or communion with his brother.

If we speak of the world today, we speak of the illusive, the incomprehensible, the stranger, the enemy, the unknown. How is it then that man does not find it more and more painful to live in such a structure? How is it that he does not lose completely the meaning of life, of true life, that is, of man himself? Why does he not seek to discover a new scale of values which would permit him to attain a style of life both contemporary and valuable?

There is much easy talk today about the sorry condition of youth. We speak of its aimless rebellion, now passive, now violent, always in anguish before the prospect of a future that holds both the worst and the best that can be imagined. There is great criticism of the iconoclastic frenzy of the young for whom "nothing is sacred," and who question the most fundamental values, whether these be moral, social, intellectual, or religious. We condemn their aimless rebellion and their ethical slackness, which border on exhibitionism and anarchy. In the upheaval of sexual norms and practice among young people, a symbol is found—perhaps correctly—of mental and social confusion. And yet, "the Establishment," having expressed its instinctive defense-reactions, is incapable of defining the content or the methodology of a new education which might prepare youth for a world that is neither absurd nor in revolt.

Society itself doubts the authenticity of its own ethic and the strength of its own philosophy. It treats today's youth like spoiled children in order not to alienate those whose rebellion already announces an uncertain future. There is a rupture between youth and society, but there is also a weakness on the part of society toward its wayward children. This is just as true in communist countries as in the free world. It occurs even at times in the Third World, once the imperatives of national emancipation assert themselves. The revolt of the world's youth everywhere illustrates the serious character and the urgency of the crisis. It underlines the two-fold nature of this crisis as one of moral consciousness and of hope.

Under these conditions, it would be inconceivable that the Church would escape the common lot of mankind. As a human community, her members share the anguish and the frustration of all men. Obviously, the ecclesial milieu as well as the milieu in which the Church exercises her ministry are both marked by the present crisis. More is to be said than this, however. The Church is also affected insofar as she is a religious institution. She is now passing through a period of uncertitude in regard to herself, in addition to that which she experiences in regard to the world.

It is often cheerfully asserted today that the Christian era is past. Gone is the time of the *corpus christianum,* inaugurated with the great Constantinian alliance between the Church and the state. The time is no more when Church and Western society—"Christian society" was the term—were looked upon as coextensive. What a sign of the times it is that we now feel such repugnance in the use of an expression which seems not only inexact but almost blasphemous. The time has passed when the proof of the "Christianization" of the world was the political and cultural dominion of the West over the rest of the world. The time has gone when the legal social order was known as "Christian" and culture had been "baptized." It is no longer an era when secular power can with impunity and at the request of the Church proceed to convert the infidels. (Think, for example, of the enforced conversion of the Jews in the Middle Ages and even at the time of the Reformation.)

However, if such times are no longer with us, it is not, alas, because the Church has spontaneously recognized her own errors. It is rather because the world, in following the logical progression of its evolution, can today get along without the Church and does not hesitate to do so. It is because the Church, formerly all-powerful, the beneficiary of privileges and exemptions, universally respected and honored, has become nothing more than a shade of her former self—an anachronism condemned by society, but more often than not simply ignored.

Because she is everywhere a minority, the Church feels threatened in her very existence. Even when census lists grant her a sociological majority, she knows well that she can no longer count on this secular power. She resides in a post- or non-Christian society, one in any case hostile or indifferent to her. It is true that there is nothing novel or surprising in this state of affairs. She has forgotten her first ages, however, with their apostolic witness, the Fathers, the persecutions, the martyrs, and the catacombs. She has forgotten that she is committed and called to be in a world which does not accept her. Because she has been established for too long a time in society, she refuses to listen to the Lord's promise: "Blessed are they who suffer persecution. . . . Happy will you be when they shall condemn you and persecute you and say all manner of things falsely against you for my sake" (Mt. 5:10-11). She has forgotten the warning: "Woe to you when they speak well of you" (Lk. 6:26).

The Church does not want to understand—does not know how to understand—that she must live each day as a constantly given gift of the Holy Spirit. She has received the promise not only of faithful, powerful witness, but of the unique possibility of life in faith and mutual love. Some few years ago, a pastor in Eastern Europe uttered these poignant words: "We must discover that the Church is to carry the Cross, but we have to do this without the strength and the joy of the Holy Spirit." Has the Spirit then abandoned us? Or has the Church perhaps doubted the Spirit, failed to ask for the Spirit, deprived herself of the Spirit without realizing it? The Church seems to count no longer on the strength of an omnipotent God, on the wisdom of an omniscient God, on the Lordship of the Master of history. Instead, she seems to prefer compromise with men in order to win their applause, and conformity which enables her to hide and forget her weakness. She has ceased to offer to the world the scandal and the folly of the Cross.

The revolution of the young is also a factor which works against the Church. It is not only an alienated world with which she must deal. Her own members turn aside from her. Let us not say that the young have always been revolutionaries, unsubmissive, rebellious; that they have always cast aside the rules of their elders and protested against the established institutions; that they have never been at ease with the heritage of the past and that their reactions should not concern us unduly, since they preserve us from immobility and ecclesiastical sclerosis. This is not so!

The revolution of youth today is much more serious. It is not simply concerned with this structure, with that organization, with Christian law or the Christian way of life. It challenges the very idea of Church and of Christian truth. It does not summon the Church to renewal. It moves ahead to leave the Church behind. It does not seek a new definition of the evangelical message. It is in search of a truth more vast, common to all men; a truth which, if it does not run counter to revelation, is at least independent of revealed truth. Think for a moment of the lack of interest on the part of young people in the ecumenical movement. In another age, youth could have been counted on for support in an effort to renew the Churches in a way that challenged the permanent quality of confessional traditions and the justice of ecclesiastical institutions. Today, a great number of the young turn aside from the ecumenical movement as such, not merely from its institutional manifestations. They reject the ecumenical activity, youth groups, Christian organizations. They demand an extension of the ecumenical movement to a point of generalization which is simply human, lacking any Christological criterion. In addition to her own uncertainties, the Church sees numerous young people challenge her identity as the Body of Christ and her vocation to witness to Jesus Christ—in a word, the ultimate criteria of her activity and her posture in the world.

With the failure of Christianity, Christians seem to have lost all ambition to create a culture, a wisdom, or an ethic significantly Christian. They seem to doubt their ability to bring effective solace to the suffering of mankind. They seem, in fact, no longer to know whether the Gospel is a burden or a source of joy, an obligation or a liberation. At the heart of a world that has no certain hope for a better future and no clear vision regarding its own meaning, the Church is meant to be a messenger of truth and of confidence. Instead, she finds refuge in timidity, silence, and false humility. She refuses to proclaim the universal royalty of Jesus Christ, under pretext of participation in his Cross. She thus fails to take part courageously in the combat for a better world. If Christians do become involved in these combats, it is as if they set aside, in so doing, their faith and their commitment to an almighty Lord. Even in their desire to share the life-condition of others through love, and to become more like these others, they have fallen prey to a deliberate conformism which affects thought and values as well as conduct.

Indeed, the Church is in the process of losing her

identity, her awareness of herself as Church situated at
the heart of the world but distinct from the world.
Among her youth and her theologians, there are some
who strive to effect a reduction of the Church to the
world, some whose efforts would achieve a complete
identification of the Church with the world. Following
the great epoch of biblical rediscovery and of Christological renewal between the twenties and the forties
of our present century, the Church seems to have undergone a period of theological confusion. A good example
of this can be found in the extraordinary success of the
book, *Honest to God* by Bishop Robinson, a prodigious
mixture of contradictory theological viewpoints borrowed from such different authors as Bonhoeffer,
Bultmann, and Tillich. It is, nevertheless, an "honest"
interrogation addressed to the contemporary Church
regarding the authenticity and the validity of her doctrine. If his theses remained unverified, Robinson's
success witnesses at least to the theological distress of
the present moment. It emphasizes the nature of this
anguish, that is, the uncertainty of the Church in regard
to the world and the responsibilities she bears toward it.

II

THEOLOGICAL CONTROVERSY

THERE IS no question of analyzing in a few pages a debate in which dogmatists, exegetes, historians, and Christian moralists are engaged today in nearly all Churches in every country. This chapter will attempt to outline some areas of discussion and research in order to determine their consequences for a Christian ethic in the contemporary world.

THE OBJECTIVITY OF SALVATION

The first point on which the current debate regarding a theology of the world bears concerns salvation and its objective character. Protestant theology still feeds in great part on the great Christocentric and Barthian affirmation borrowed from the sixteenth-century Reformers. Contrary to human wisdom and natural religion, salvation is not a work to be accomplished, even with the help of God and by his grace. It is not a transformation to be realized, either in terms of eternal destiny or in those of daily existence. Salvation *is,* in the strongest sense of the word, Jesus Christ. It manifests the character of an irrevocable historical accomplishment. It proceeds from the initiative of God alone and of the gracious gift which he has given to all men without any merit on their part. Salvation is the central event of history, the ultimate reality of the world. If it is still to be shown forth in a glory to come, it is not for that less real. Nothing can ever annul it.

This might sound very much like theological universalism. These definitions, however, preserve a strictly Christological basis and reject all optimistic idealism. If we are resolutely optimistic regarding the salvation of mankind, it is because of Jesus Christ alone. If we do not speak of universal salvation, it is because we refuse to set ourselves up as masters of salvation instead of accepting the fact that we are unworthy beneficiaries of this gift. We refuse to move from the free love of God to a cosmological system. This in no way lessens the truth that the last word of all is the love of God, from which nothing can separate us (Rom. 8:39) and the peace of God which is stronger than all our doubts and anxieties (Phil. 4:7). In a word, we are not asked to affirm or reject the universality of salvation. We are asked to believe in the limitless love of the Savior.

However that may be, what has been said above can still give an impression of universalism without saying anything at all about the necessity of witness, of conversion, or even of faith. If all men are recipients of the redemptive work of Jesus Christ, why wear ourselves out in preaching? Why summon constantly to repentance and to belief? Why, furthermore, condemn the syncretic forms of belief into which men at all times stray, since the infidelity of men can never annul the fidelity of God (2 Tim. 2:13)? These questions often provoke violent reactions on the part of both conservative and progressive theologians. They easily find biblical and patristic texts to condemn the indifferentism to which a consistent universalism leads. Since this problem is erroneous in its premises, however, anyone who takes it seriously runs the risk of falling into contrary errors, just as pernicious as those avoided.

The universalist error seems to be that of substituting a cosmological system for the free grace of God. The opposing error consists in restoring a theology of merit, in an effort to struggle against the pseudo-universalism of the Gospel, and in perverting the Gospel into militant proselytism in order to justify the notion of mission. In both instances, man is substituted for God either as author of a system of general salvation or as the one who brings about his own personal salvation.

In one instance and the other, furthermore, a theology of the world is enunciated implicitly in such a way as to make of the world an autonomous reality in regard to God. From a universalistic point of view, the world —automatically or, it might be said, ontologically— destined for salvation, has no need of a God who can no longer be our interlocuter, since he has been reduced to a salutary mechanism. As for the Church, it has no living head and so becomes a kind of comfortable club where men, content with the prospects of the future and free from problems of conscience, reunite from time to time to congratulate one another on having chosen to live in the best of all worlds. From the point of view of merit and proselytism, too, the world can manage quite well without God. As the domain of evil and of nothingness, the world is that from which one escapes in pure negativity, that from which the Church isolates herself and against which she builds up protecting barricades.

These two antagonistic attitudes, as simplistic as they may seem in caricature, are not for all that totally excluded from the preaching, the teaching, and the activity of the Churches. Flowing from a faulty interpretation of the historical objectivity of salvation as affirmed in

Scripture, they testify to the seriousness of our present theological chaos. There is no other means of escaping from the falsity of either alternative except the Gospel itself as it proclaims the historicity of the Savior and his work. Belief in him is neither adherence to a body of doctrines nor meriting a regenerative pardon. To believe in him is to live with him in a vital, vivifying relationship. When we preach Jesus Christ, we do not ask for a spiritual or moral transformation of which men are incapable. We do not ask for adhesion to a Church which seldom evokes the image of her Lord. Rather, we offer them *hic et nunc* the joy of the Gospel, the inebriating liberty of a life without fear of the morrow or remorse for the past. We offer them a life without terror of judgment, a life which is mortal, but free from any trace of the suffocating odor of death.

In this perspective, the salvation of the world should no longer be merely on object of interesting cosmological speculation. It is the splended gift offered to all even before they are aware of it. We no longer bear witness in order to save men, but in order that Jesus Christ, their Savior, may be their full joy. We no longer stand in horror of the world, since the promise of the Savior is given to all and we cannot despise what he has so loved (Jn. 3:16). It would be otherwise if the work of Jesus Christ were not an objective, ultimate achievement. It would be otherwise if salvation were simply a matter of involvement or of existential experience. If there were no other reality than that known in the lives of men, the world would be either an enemy threatening to stand in the way of human involvement and experience or the totally human source and content of this involvement and experience. Under such conditions, we would be hopelessly imprisoned in a closed world with no other reality than ourselves. Some contemporary "theologians" dare to say that "God is dead." If they think this is so, is it not because Christians "kill" him by enclosing themselves in the world? The Gospel has another message as it proclaims that through the death of the Son of God on Golgotha, the world has been opened forever into the eternal life of the Resurrection.

DESACRALIZATION OF THE WORLD

As popular as it was at the beginning of the century, the notion of the "sacred" is on the verge of being banished from Christian thought. Dietrich Bonhoeffer was one of the first to denounce "religion." This German Protestant theologian, executed in 1945, in his last letters from prison attacked the sacred in a more provocative manner than anyone had until that time. For him, "religion" and the sacred were the instruments employed by the Church to keep the world in a state of subjection when it had already come of age and was "adult." According to Bonhoeffer, "we cannot be honest with ourselves unless we recognize that we must live in the world *etsi Deus non daretur*; not as unbelievers, but 'before God and with God.' We must experience the absence of God who abandons us (Mk. 15:34), of God who has chosen to be feeble and weak in a strong world." Only then can he help us, not "by his omnipotence, but by his weakness and his sufferings." In a word, Bonhoeffer saw that the world, in coming of age, had rid itself of a "false image of God," the image of the sacred, of the deus ex machina.

In thus repudiating the notion of the "religious," Bonhoeffer restored the value of the world in its worldliness. In revealing the naked truth of the humanity of God in Jesus Christ, Bonhoeffer eliminated the profane veneer by which religion had disguised God. He delivered the world from the yoke imposed on it by a "sacred" which had originally come forth from the world but which had since fallen into sterile dialogue with it.

With the elimination of the religious, the world as the authentic profane reality recovers the freedom of being able to dialogue with God.

The theological proposition of Bonhoeffer is simple, but the immense consequences of this proposition have yet to be adequately explored. On a strictly doctrinal level, Bonhoeffer, like his master Barth (from whom, however, he differs on several points), emphasizes the vanity of any ontological definition of God. He stresses the inadequacy of borrowing attributes from the world, even in negative terms, to qualify God as infinite, eternal, perfect, holy. God is absent from the world because he is other than the world. Thus, he cannot be demonstrated or known by means of science, philosophy, art, or culture. Every human vocabulary is inadequate here. He is other, yet he is present—present in Jesus Christ. He is not of the world, but has freely assumed human nature. We know God in misery, incognito, in his humanity and nowhere else. Useless and vain, then, are the syncretic apologetics and assimilations which attempt to reduce God to nothing more than the "better part" of this world.

At the historical level, Bonhoeffer restores the meaning of human history. On this point, however, the work of Arend Th. van Leeuwen is more recent. In a detailed analysis (in *Christianity in World History,* Scribner's, 1966), he describes the gradual emancipation of the world from the "ontocratic" yoke of a sacralized nature. This occurred first of all under the shock of Israel's influence. Then the Church and Christianity accentuated the theocratic character of the world. The world no longer belonged to a sacred order, because God alone is holy. Nature, society, the state, and culture are essentially profane, thus temporal, human, and called to become ever more "human."

If Christianity is historically responsible for the

appearance of this revolutionary ferment, the Church
has too often yielded to the temptations of the sacred.
She has established herself in Christianity, that is, in a
sacred institution and civilization, contrary to the very
genius of the Christian faith. The heritage has been
taken up in the hands of Western technical civilization
and its profane notion of man and his collective future.
For this reason, van Leeuwen plays the part of a fervent
advocate of the secularity of the state, of society, and
of culture. He attributes to the Church the duty of
upholding this secularity. In a word, the Church must
not attempt to Christianize and sacralize the world. She
must desacralize it in order to be free to transform it,
according to the will of God, for the good of humanity.

It is not possible to present more details from this
extraordinary book with its lucid arguments and multiple
concrete references. There is no ambiguity about its
major thesis: Religion as a collective expression of the
sacred is a contradiction of the Christian faith; the
Church must support and share in the modern secularization of civilization as fruit of the biblical revelation.
It is not possible to rehabilitate the world in a better
manner than by restoring its autonomy in regard to
the religious and its dependence on him who is its
creator, its preserver, its destiny.

Critics of Bonhoeffer and van Leeuwen are not lacking. Many ask, for example, if van Leeuwen does not
conclude to a curious sacralization of the secular. Does
he still have the right to speak of the "theocratic" when
Western technical civilization deliberately sets aside
all reference to God or to Jesus Christ? Are we not
dealing here with a new "ontocratic" category in which
history, revolution, and progress are sacralized? Does
the Church still have an original message to proclaim in
the daily fulfillment of her ministry? Does her community still exhibit any distinct quality and, if not, can

she still be recognized as the Body of Christ?

However all this may be, a major question has been asked of the Church. Does not the evolution of the world and its lack of interest in the Gospel reflect the reality of human sin? Or is this situation to be looked upon as the judgment of God in condemnation of the infidelity of his Church? The answer to these questions can be found only through a systematic, open theological study of the world. Until this is done, it is essential to listen to the question which the world addresses to the Church. For the world is not only the questioner to be met in the bearing of witness; it is also, perhaps, a messenger bearing the word of the Lord.

THEOLOGY OF HISTORY: DISCERNING THE SIGNS

Van Leeuwen concentrates on the historical, anti-naturalistic character of revelation, following the quasi-consensus of Protestant theology. The Lordship of Jesus Christ is an historical fact, founded on an event which can be given a date. This event affects the totality of history from the creation of the world to its ultimate fulfillment. There is no autonomous theology of creation as distinct from a theology of redemption. The Lord Jesus, master of history, is also master of nature. His miracles witness to this. The New Testament affirms his role as creator (Jn. 1:3). In the same way, there is no separation between the vocation of man and the historical vocation of the Church. Man is to dominate, cultivate, and understand the whole of nature. The Church is to proclaim the Gospel and to present a living witness of it to the world. There is no room for two realities in the world: one, physical, material, non-historical, the other intellectual, spiritual, uniquely historical. The world is one because the same Lord created it, saved it, and at the end-time will renew it in full perfection.

Furthermore, there is a continuity of history. This is not an element introduced by men, but pertains to the will of God. Here, a problem presents itself. Is it possible for us to know the acts of the Lord God of History, other than those in which he has revealed himself in normative fashion in the biblical accounts? Does our interregnum situation constrain us to respect the mystery of history whose key is held only by the Father (Acts 1:7)? Should we, following what seems to be the New Testament challenge, make an effort to "discern the signs of the times" (Lk. 12:56)? Or is this text in Luke restricted to the one "true sign," the incarnation of Jesus Christ? Must history, then, under the Lordship of Jesus Christ, remain forever indecipherable?

There have always been philosophers or historians who judge that history is unintelligible. They see in it only a chaotic maelstrom of individual and collective energies conflicting in a purely biological and irrational development. At the heart of this chaos are men, who attempt to organize themselves through recourse to the great collective myths, more often than not borrowed from the natural order. On the contrary, Christian theology has always affirmed the intelligibility of history as the locus of the redemptive work of Jesus Christ and the object of his love. History is intelligible because of its aim, its goal, its end, and not by reason of its nature or essence. If God acts mysteriously in history, we know through faith that he is history's end. If God is invisible in history, he is not absent from it. History is never abandoned to itself. The world has an historical meaning and a direction: Jesus Christ, the same at the end of historical time as he was in his incarnation.

If the ultimate sources of the divine history of the world remain hidden from us, history is still intelligible because it constitutes the field of our service. There is no normative reading of history; there is a reading, however, imperative for each of us—our vocation. The object of this vocation is to insert us into history—and into the world's history—as representatives (ambassadors, says Paul) of the universal Lord. This vocation frees us for a history whose fatalities we recognize as so many deceptive appearances, because the future of this history is the Kingdom. This vocation summons us to be responsible for history, bearing the burden of orienting it toward its authentic and proper end. We are called to be revolutionaries in an historical dimension which is never adequate to its destiny. We are asked above all to be patient with history, because it is the history of a world which God loves.

In an attempt to be more precise, can we define a Christian program of action in history? The task is difficult. The signs of the times require a decodification which comprises in part a technical analysis. And the specialists are not always in agreement over the rules governing this analysis. Thus, discernment becomes a relative matter. It is relative, first, in terms of what concerns the immediate moment in a world in constant evolution. It is relative in view of the human mind which cannot embrace the immense complexity of factors determining history and each of its events in the twinkling of an eye. It is relative, finally, because all interpretations are diverse rather than unanimous. In all humility, their temporary, pragmatic character must be admitted. An effort must be made toward mutual correction so that a clearer vision will be attained and a deeper comprehension reached. As relative as these attempts at discernment are, they agree in looking upon the world as the domain of God, the place of his activity, the site of our vocation. They recognize, as it were, the "eminent dignity" of this world. Is there, then, theological agreement in this matter? Far from it.

Nowhere can more violent disagreement and more

antagonistic concepts be found than in attempts to define history. In general, it might be said that apocalyptic theologies, dualistic and sectarian in tendency, are set up in opposition to eschatological theologies which deny any absolute rupture between God and the world and which, consequently, remain open to the world. Apocalyptic theologies are dualistic insofar as they attribute to the world and to Satan, the prince of this world, an autonomous power. Thus they deny that "all power, all authority, all sovereignty" have been forever subjected to the Lord Jesus Christ (Eph. 1:21). They look upon actual history as a conflict which will issue certainly in the catastrophic annihilation of the world. For this reason, the Church must carefully hold herself apart from the world in an authentic phariseeism. Her aim must be to snatch from the world, that is from annihilation, as many men as possible. She has no need to be concerned with the world, its history, or its civilization. She must, on the contrary, fight to condemn these things and pursue her missionary efforts to rescue the small number who will be saved. In order to preserve the Church from the world, all doors which lead to it must be closed. She must isolate herself in a ghetto and struggle diligently against heresy and the intrusion of the profane into the sacred. She must chase away evil within and without and refuse all part with ecumenism, since this implies an openness beyond her dogmatic orthodoxy.

Eschatological theologies are those which see the world as redeemed by Jesus Christ. They look upon it as destined not for annihilation but for regeneration and for re-creation in perfection. It follows that every historical moment can have a positive meaning, in view of a future of light and joy. This is no idealistic optimism counting on intrinsically human capacities for progress. This assurance is founded entirely on the certitude that

Jesus Christ is Lord of all history, therefore of its last and final realization. In this perspective, every historical event, every human effort, all expectation and hope have a meaning. They constitute a vocation in that they represent the possibility of action to make this world what it is now only in a hidden way: the royal domain of Jesus Christ.

The ministry of the Church is not meant to separate men from their humanity or from their "laicity." She calls them to act in the economic, social, cultural, and scientific fields in order to produce in the world the fruits that God expects of it. The community of the Church is fully open, ready for dialogue and eager to welcome all who come to her. She does not tremble at the threat of heresy, because she knows that the world is not the enemy of the Lord but his secret instrument. She knows that all wicked powers at work within the world are already vanquished. Here we have a profound optimism, one which does not count on eventual triumph, but which relies on the certitude that, objectively, "all is consummated" by the Lord of love, even here and now.

The limits of this chapter have permitted only a sketch of some of the contemporary themes in theological reflection and an indication of the way in which they focus on the problem of the significance of the world for the Church. From this outline, it is clear that the notion of the world is inevitably projected into involvement in the world by the activity of the Church or of the Christian. Theological options determine practical decisions. It is necessary now to describe or more exactly to suggest some directives flowing from contemporary ecumenical experience according to which a new ethic seems to be developing on the part of the Church in the world.

III

REVOLUTION
AND RECONCILIATION

A BIBLICAL theology of history excludes systematic progress. It is not less true that the vocation of the Church in the world is one of progress. By this is meant that the Church must struggle against everything which would destroy the work of God and must contribute to every human effort that would restore the primordial integrity of creation or the image of its ultimate regeneration, no matter how imperfectly this is done. From this point of view, our task can be seen as one of revolution and reconciliation. Our vocation is one of revolution, for the results acquired and the situation established will never correspond adequately to the Kingdom which is the destiny of the world. There will always be evil, injustice, oppression, ugliness, and imperfection to denounce and oppose. We will never be allowed to indulge in complacency or satisfaction. The watchwords of the Christian are: purification, regeneration, reconstruction, revolution.

Our vocation is also one of reconciliation. In his grace, God has decided to spare us the chastisement merited by our infidelity. After the Fall, Adam and Eve received the promise of salvation, even though they were expelled from Paradise. Cain, the murderer, fled from the face of God marked by a sign of protection. The rainbow witnessed to the fact that the purifying deluge would never again take place. The Lord God, jealous of his own power, brought ruin on the Promethean tower of Babel and dispersed the nations in a confusion of tongues. He extended to them also, however, the promise made to Abraham. Again and again, God forgave the rebellion of Israel and renewed his covenant with her. "In the very place where it is said, 'You are not my people,' it will be said, 'You are sons of the living God'" (Osee 1:10). Finally, Jesus Christ, eternal Son of God, bears the weight of our rebellion and delivers us from eternal condemnation by the Holy of Holies. By his sacrifice, he destroys the walls which separate us one from another. In him reconciliation is more than a promise or a vocation. It becomes an historical reality, the basis and the criterion of our obedience.

How is it possible to combine these two apparently contradictory positions? How can we live as revolutionaries, as puritans, with the necessary implicit terrorism demanded by this character, and at the same time practice patience, meekness, forgiveness, and the fraternal love shown by the Savior of Golgotha? If we attempt to synthesize the two systems, we find ourselves very quickly blocked by a logical impossibility because, in reality, we are faced by two antagonistic exigencies. There is but one solution to the problem: Jesus Christ, himself. He became a victim of the holiness of God for love of us; he underwent and continues to undergo chastisement for us. We are not called to revolution as a matter of principle, or to reconciliation at any price. We are called to believe in and to live in Jesus Christ. This is a situation which is perhaps logically and humanly difficult, but it is spiritually authentic. In other words, our task of reconciliation constitutes at all times the limit of our revolutionary obligations and the work of revolution which is ours determines the extent of our responsibilities in reconciliation. As witnesses, we must be intransigent in our fidelity, even while fraternal love helps us to understand, to wait patiently, to make no demands. We must be jealous for God's truth which binds us together; we must be equally jealous for the efficacy of our service to men. We cannot condemn the world in the name of the sanctity of God anymore than we can remain indifferent to its imperfections and its vices. We have no right to destroy the world under pretext of purifying it. We are not permitted to love it without striving to contribute toward its regeneration.

Perhaps the best word to describe this dialectic between revolution and reconciliation is one which enjoys great popularity at the present moment, having come out of the difficulties experienced by the Church in the East German Democratic Republic: pro-existence. If we are called to pro-existence, it is because we cannot find the reason and the criterion of our existence in ourselves, but only in God and in our fellow men. We live in order to adore God and to love our neighbor in self-forgetfulness. We must know how to sacrifice everything in order to give witness to the demanding holiness of the Eternal God. Following the example of our Lord Jesus Christ, we must learn to sacrifice ourselves and not others. In serving men as they are, we bear authentic witness to the God whose sanctity is one with his love.

IN THE CHURCH

Everyone knows today that unity of the Church and
Church renewal are interdependent, like the two poles
of ecumenical reflection and action. The division of the
Church is a striking manifestation of sin, for sin always
contributes to this division. Consequently, there is prac-
tically speaking no path to unity which does not travel
through renewal of the Church and each of her members, that is, through repentance and conversion. If
unity could be achieved through some subtle compromise by which the old theological separations and
historical antagonisms might be overcome, the Church-
made-one through such efforts would certainly present
an imposing image to the world. She would even manifest a certain efficacy in her activities. But she would
no longer be the Church of Jesus Christ, crucified Lord,
who chooses "the weak things of this world." She would
be a magnificent human structure, without any value
because she would be exclusively human. We must, on
the contrary, never cease to remind ourselves that the
unity of the Church demands renunciation on her part.
She must abandon her most precious human possessions
and historical traditions (but never the truth of the
Gospel which is, in any case, not possessed but which
possesses her). A few years ago, the leader of one
Church, in speaking of the ecumenical effort which
seems at times to move so slowly and in which each
Church manifests so meager a spirit of renunciation,
proposed the following comparison:

> Our Churches are like two friends who set out separ-
> ately on a trip, each one laden with a heavy suitcase
> containing his most precious possessions. They meet on
> opposite sides of a deep chasm, so wide that they can-
> not cross it without leaving their suitcases behind. Each
> one cries out to the other, "Come on over! Don't worry
> about your luggage. I have enough here for both of us."

The dialogue might go on indefinitely. There is, however, another possible solution. Both friends could jump together, with their suitcases, each toward the other, and meet at the bottom of the chasm—a chasm so deep that the leap costs both of them their lives. The story would be senseless, except that we are speaking now of the Church of Jesus Christ and that we believe that it is in dying that the grain of wheat bears much fruit.

If unity is to be achieved through repentance and renunciation, it is also a factor in the renewal it promises. The contemporary ecumenical movement proceeds directly from the great missionary awakening of the nineteenth centry. It has also led to a universal missionary effort. It is remarkable that the World Council of Churches united in 1961 with the International Council of the Missions and undertook the systematic study of the "missionary structures" necessary for the Church to accomplish her apostolic vocation. As she prepares and realizes her unity, the Church must take care that she is not doing more than assuring the solidity of the bonds which unite her members. Above all, she must achieve an efficacious contact with the exterior world and with humanity, to whom her witness is due.

If there is interdependence between unity and renewal, there is just as surely tension between these two elements. This tension leads us to the revolution-reconciliation dialectic. That is why the ecumenical movement, which is authentically revolutionary, cannot avoid taking an institutional form even though, in so doing, the revolutionary character is with difficulty maintained. That is why the Protestant Churches, attached as they are to the formula *ecclesia reformata quia semper reformanda,* are not the last to emphasize the value and the importance of tradition. The debates at the Conference on Faith and Order at Montreal in 1963 showed this clearly. All our Churches without exception must face the apparently insoluble problem between authority and liberty. Beneath all the conflicts lies the same fundamental opposition between reconciliation with its concern for peace and unity and revolution with its stress on purity and renewal.

More precise examples of this dialectical tendency can be found in present-day ecumenical problems. There are those, for example, who would realize a unity of action in terms of effective, practical application of theory. Others are more oriented toward organic, doctrinal unity. Young Christian revolutionaries want to arrive at results without passing through prior stages. On another level, there is the question of the "ecclesial" character of the united activity found in such conciliar structures as the World Council of Churches or similar national and regional councils. Again, there are those adherents of local unity, who hold that collaboration is to be achieved within the limits and in terms of contemporary world problems. These persons are opposed by others who think in terms of confessional unity, to be realized in a continuity of theological, institutional tradition. At times, it seems that the desire to resolve theological problems of the past threatens to delay or even to hinder present-day unity. At other times, it might validly be asked whether unity accomplished simply in virtue of today's problems will not degenerate into some cultural, social, or political organization rather than develop into a Christian assembly.

It must be repeatedly stressed that there is no theoretical solution to the dilemma. Only through a living relation with Jesus Christ in faith and prayer can there be found the basis for hope to bring about both unity of the Church and Church renewal. The only real danger consists in locking ourselves within ecclesiastical pride, in counting on our strengths, in seeking unity or renewal for selfish purposes, without humility and love. In other words, there will be no unity or renewal for the Church

except in Jesus Christ and through his grace. This
implies that both unity and renewal will be found only
in service of the world and in an authentic, humble participation in its daily reality.

IN POLITICS

In this area, the dialectical opposition between revolution and reconciliation becomes the tension between
order and justice. Here, great care must be taken not to
introduce an over-simplified equation of justice and love.
True order proceeds from an authentic love of humanity
which strives to assure to man the conditions necessary
for peaceful, tranquil existence (1 Tim. 2:2). True
order corresponds to the reconciling design of God to
the degree that it prevents men from destroying one
another.

On the contrary, it is evident that, even under this
positive aspect, order can become an obstacle to any
political renewal. In the world today, it also becomes,
in consequence of this, an obstacle to the service of
humanity whose sufferings are more often than not the
result of collective political causes. That is why politics
provides a language for Christian witness and a vocabulary for reference to the otherness of the Kingdom of
God. The life of the Kingdom is not only a life of
personal renewal for each man individually. It is a life
of struggle to renew the structures of society. Today,
as in the time of the prophets of the Old Testament, the
holiness of God calls for collective purification of the
people.

The life of the Kingdom also consists in the concrete,
effective service of men. The Christian is not to be concerned primarily with the success of some system, of
a given party, of this or that ideology. He is not called
to love mankind tomorrow; he is challenged to love his
neighbor today. A Christian, then, can never sincerely

justify the evils of war or revolution in the name of the benefits they may eventually bring about. The Christian is constantly torn between his duty to act in an effective manner, thus granting priority to the results of collective action, and the sacred character which love of Jesus Christ confers on each unique person. More than this, the Christian must renounce any notion of the *corpus christianum* which would absolutize the priority of efficacious action by identifying it with God's truth, as well as a Christian progressivism which would justify revolutionary violence by pointing to a hypothetical future when perfect happiness will be available for all. Such attitudes manifest themselves in the kind of political Catholicism which seems to have been definitely condemned by Vatican Council II or in Marxist Communism which in many ways, in the last analysis, is a Christian heresy.

A concrete example of the principle under discussion can be found in the contemporary racial problem. Too often, the Church is content with impressive theoretical declarations which condemn racism and exhort all Christians to foster true equality among the races. Too often she limits her action in this matter to a charity which is certainly to be praised, but which does not come to grips with difficult political conflicts. Would it not be better for our Churches to begin with a serious examination of conscience and an effort to live out their ecclesial existence by following Jesus Christ? This would entail interior reform and a categorical dismissal of all forms of ecclesiastical racial segregation. Indeed, can any Church claim to bear the name of Christ as long as she bears the signs of those distinctions between Greek and Jew, barbarian, slave, and free for which the entire New Testament tells us there is no longer any place? Perhaps it must be by means of an intransigent attitude toward themselves and severity toward members unfaithful in this domain that the Churches will be able to give to the world, imprisoned in its prejudices, the example of authentic liberty and justice and the proof that these truths can be attained. It may be in this way, also, that the Church will most clearly demonstrate the nature of that ministry of reconciliation which she is summoned to bear, in witness to the one and only true Reconciler. The Church will manifest the deepest compassion toward all victims of racism not only by her own repentance, but by calling upon herself the wrath of persecutors. Ultimately, the task of the Church in the world is to bear the Cross of Calvary with all victims before she can act in the name of the victorious Lord of the Resurrection.

In the domain of politics, however, direct action is not always to be avoided. In a particularly painful manner, it will always provoke the revolution-reconciliation dilemma, most markedly in the form of the eternal question of the legitimacy of violence. There is not one Christian who escapes the temptation either to reject all violence as contradictory to the love of Jesus Christ or to espouse violence because without it we become the accomplices of injustice and disorder. The word "temptation" is significant in this context. It is always a temptation to try to reduce everything to a simple answer and to forget some aspect of what our faith demands of us.

Once again, it must be stated that there can be no principle of solution, no magic formula to be applied to suppress the alternatives. Our human condition and our participation in a fallen world will never allow us to have a perfectly clear conscience or totally innocent hands. The blood of Abel and the blood of Jesus Christ are upon us, along with the blood of all the human victims whom we abandon to their own destiny so that we can be free to be worthy of our God. When we strike the robbers whom Christ pardoned, we renounce and deny his blood. We can only surrender ourselves to Jesus Christ, the Savior, who pardons all men, no matter what their intent. He has taken the place of every victim from Abel the just down to the Negroes of South Africa and Alabama. What more is there to say? In each particular instance, we must assume the risks with the responsibilities, knowing that we are accountable for our brothers. We must be guided in our action by the justice, liberty, and happiness which God wills for men. In the pardon of God, on which we rely, there must be no excuse for a failure to act, but an added motive for full involvement as we go forward courageously and efficaciously into the world's combats.

There is one further word to be said concerning today's racial conflicts. Is it necessary to employ the intervention of foreign military power or varied techniques of revolution and guerrilla resistance to bring to an end in South Africa a political system of oppression, exploitation, and degradation? Perhaps we can not exclude such a possibility until we can be certain of being able to use successfully other, nonviolent measures. The legitimacy of this principle, however, cannot be imposed by decree. The reason for this position rests not in a desire to avoid giving scandal to some of our brothers in the faith, since others would be scandalized were the contrary position adopted. This attitude, rather, is dictated by Christian wisdom, which prompts us never to abandon hope of peaceful solution, but to return constantly in all honesty to a serious study of the actual evolving condition of any conflict. It is conceivable, also, that different attitudes on the part of Christians toward similar problems can be found in different parts of the world, without introducing any trace of incoherence into the Christian posture, for no two conflicts are ever exactly the same. Finally, the witness of those who refuse any part with violence must not be excluded. Those who claim to be "conscientious objectors" suffer as a result of their choice. If, in certain instances, they seem to enjoy some personal privilege as a consequence of their objection, they are the first to suffer from this.

IN INTERNATIONAL AFFAIRS

In this domain, the dialectic we have been discussing comprises peace and law (or justice). Peace corresponds to reconciliation, while law corresponds to revolution. By law is meant the maintenance of right over disorder, the domination of a juridically established justice against the domination of might. Tension is thus set up between the establishment of peace, without which humanity is threatened with annihilation, and of law, without which human existence can deteriorate into anarchical animality. Before Hiroshima, the problem was less complex than it is today. Even during the Second World War, it was possible to think in terms of a just (or justifiable) war, because the responsible heads of states could honestly perceive in this means a way of bettering the lot of the human race. Nuclear weapons have changed the facts of the problem. What betterment can ever come out of a holocaust? No matter what political position one adopts on the question, one is immediately up against the fundamental conflict between revolutionary justice and peaceful reconciliation. The pacifists are just as revolutionary as those who formulate the theories of international justice. One and the other reject the conservatism of the established order. All are equally desirous for peace and for a liquidation of the injustices inflicted on suffering peoples. This is true even in the communist world, which is often accused of seeking nothing more than the advantages of political propagandizing.

Among the vastly differentiated problems presented to the Church in virtue of international relations, two are especially significant.

1. The peace involved here is the human, secular transposition of the work of reconciliation effected by Jesus Christ, prince of peace. What form should this peace take at the present moment in history? More particularly, what are we to think today of one widely-known concept, that of peaceful coexistence? Coexistence is different from justice and peace, but perhaps it constitutes a good balance between the two. It does not assure peace, but prevents war. It does not achieve perfect justice, but sets limits to injustice. A priori, it seems to be a compromise solution, satisfying insofar as it corresponds in some degree to the contradictory preoccupations of peace and justice. Furthermore, it constitutes a necessary minimum with which we must not be satisfied. We must accept the challenge to make coexistence increasingly peaceful, increasingly like both peace and justice. In other words, from the passive stance of coexistence, we must seek unceasingly to move to the active posture of dialogue and collaboration between powers and ideologies in view of serving together all those who need our assistance.

2. A second central problem is that of the equitable distribution of resources among nations, along with the economic development of underdeveloped countries. More and more, it is the man on the street who is as aware as the experts that the crucial political question of our age lies in this area. Justice no longer is a matter of classes, as in the last century, but of nations and, unfortunately at times, of races. In the current meaning of the word, revolution is no longer exclusively a social

matter, but has taken on an international dimension. The Latin American continent which has been the victim of repeated revolutionary upheavals knows only too well that substantial social transformation and any progress in justice must involve a radical revision of its dealings with the United States. The problem of justice thus becomes a question of peace. Events in Cuba and the Dominican Republic have testified only too well that economic and social transformations do not provoke political disturbances alone. They also induce an acute international tension. As much might be said for the crises afflicting Asia and Africa. We are living in an era in which every political event has immedate international repercussions. The question of the legitimacy of violence is raised no longer in the context of the traditional revolutionary problematic, but against the background of the atomic spectre.

It becomes impossible, then, in this area as in the others considered above, to find a solution simply by recognizing the rights of revolutionaries to defend the hungry and the oppressed. Revolution and reconciliation cannot be sacrificed, one to the other. As a method of international procedure, negotiation assumes another aspect and the role of the United Nations takes on new proportions. As in the case of racism, the role of the Church becomes one of giving an example of renunciation and of purification. What more meaningful manner of contributing to the struggle for international justice than that of sacrificing the wealth which we Christians so often control, especially in the West? This sacrifice could be made for the benefit of the young Churches and even the inhabitants of the Third World. Why do the Churches of the West not make a greater effort—for they do strive to do this on a small scale—to assist the Third World by giving their money, their time, and above all their specialists and experts to maintain and foster every form of economic and social development sought by that world?

IN CULTURAL LIFE

If the motif of revolution is more predominant on the political and international levels, the accent in the domain of culture must be placed on the theme of reconciliation. When we speak of culture, we speak of communication between men and of the language needed for life in common. At the present time, we are experiencing a period of crisis in culture. This is an age in which men unlearn language and rely on instruments of communication which do not appeal in so direct a way to the intelligence and to reason. They have recourse to instruments of communication which belong rather to the semiautomatic, subrational dimension, whether in political propaganda, commercial publicity, or, even, at times, pedagogy. The degree to which the decadence of language and of culture has progressed is highly disputed. At any rate, the danger is a real one.

Language is not merely indispensable for life in society. It is necessary for the witness of the Church. As the body of Christ, eternal Word of God, the Church has the mission of proclaiming this Word. It is not possible to express the eternal Word except in human words. Thus, a culture must be utilized and shared for the accomplishment of this ministry. When this culture is still in an embryonic state, it is inadequate or it contradicts the essence of the message it bears. Then the Church is led to become the creator of a culture.

Is it possible, though, to create a culture *ex nihilo*? Is this not an ambition which exceeds its possibilities? The past furnishes us with more than one example of the role which Christianity has played in this area. One that is well-known is that of the confrontation, both religious and cultural, between the Christian faith and hellenistic civilization in the first centuries of our era. We know in what way the sometimes initial contact of the revolutionary message of the Gospel effected a veritable transmutation of the values of this civilization. It would be an exaggeration, however, to speak here of a cultural "creation"; the civilization of Augustine and the great Eastern Fathers of the fourth and fifth centuries simply continued the classical Mediterranean civilization.

The Syrian phenomenon furnishes a still better example of cultural creation in the strict sense of the term. If the Moslem invasions had not severed the relations of the Syrian world with the rest of Christianity; if Syrian culture had not been destroyed during the Turkish period, this astonishing civilization which had been born out of the Christian mission in the third century would never have fallen into oblivion, as it has today. Here there was truly a Christian civilization, not in the Western sense of the word, which refers rather to a predominance of values issuing from Christianity itself or from relations between the Church and society. This civilization was Christian in the broader meaning of having been truly engendered by the truths of revelation, by theology, and by the ecclesial community.

The Syrian language even developed as a cultural language after or, more precisely, parallel to the conversion of the peoples of Syro-Mesopotamia. Architecture, music—a total aesthetic proceeded directly from the life of the Church and later influenced Islam and the Byzantine world. From the fourth century on, institutions of learning presented in their structures, their programs, and their pedagogy many of the future traits of the medieval universities of the West. It is highly probable that a real transmission of this pre-university concept to Western Europe was effected through Arab civilization, elaborated by the Syrian professors of

Edessa, Nisibis and Seleucia-Ctesiphon. In these Syrian schools, it is true, the results of Greek philosophy and science were employed, along with the fruits of Eastern theology. At an epoch, however, when the Mediterranean world still held to the classical pattern of education, the directors of these schools elaborated a new pedagogy. They were among the first Christian thinkers to conceive of scientific research as a Christian vocation. This brief summary will suffice to indicate that the creation of culture is not an impossibility for Christian faith.

There is something more to be said, however. In these Syrian schools, knowledge was looked upon under an eminently utilitarian aspect. Here were formed priests who were to direct and teach the Church. Here were prepared men of science who were not to limit themselves to research, but who would be excellent practitioners of many skills. Here were fostered artists who not only created liturgy but gave expression to the aesthetic sense of Syrian society. Above all, here were formed the pedagogues who would disseminate methodology as well as knowledge and thus contribute to the building up of society.

It would obviously be absurd to try to repeat the Syrian experience. This culture was born out of the initiative and the inspiration of the Church. If this was possible, it was because Christianity coming to birth in the Syro-Mesopotamian atmosphere found itself in a cultural void, relatively speaking. With the Gospel, however, Christianity had inherited a rich intellectual, moral, and aesthetic tradition from the people of Israe and, in a large degree, from the hellenistic world. Per haps the next stage in the cultural history of Syria can lead us to useful practical conclusions. Even when cu off from its contacts with Mediterranean Christianit and, soon afterwards, from the outlying posts of merid ional, central, and eastern Asia, Syrian Christianity was still able to survive. In the first centuries of Moslem domination, Syrian culture experienced not a decadence but a flowering. In fact, once the bonds established between the Church, culture, and society were broken, even under the Iranian domination of the Sassanids, Syrian culture manifested its facility for adaptation.

Once Christians and Moslems began to associate within the same society, Syrian culture became common to two religious worlds which, at that time, were in bitter conflict everywhere. While Christian and Moslem armies fought on Eastern and Western fronts throughout the long years of Moslem conquest and Christian reconquest, the Syrian world preserved its cultural homogeneity. It served as the bridge between Islam and Christianity. The majority of Syrian intellectuals were Christians, but they taught their wisdom and their knowledge to Moslems. They assured the translation of the Greek classics, first of all into Syriac, then into Arabic. This is one of the paths by which Aristotle came to the West. It was the great Turkish catastrophe which was to ruin Syrian culture at the same time that it destroyed Arabic culture.

In other words, Syrian culture, born as it was of the Christian faith, was able to maintain an authentic communication between Christians and Moslems, even in its contact with a religion as exclusive as Islam. Thus it gives an example of the possibility for Christians and for the Church to maintain men and societies in dialogue on a cultural plane. Much openness of mind and spirit is needed, with great flexibility in regard to the concepts, opinions, and knowledge of others. In the last analysis, this must be the guiding principle: *Nil humani a me alienum.* A Church which is closed in upon itself, a science and culture constructed around intangible dogmas—these can no longer furnish men with instruments of communication necessary for dialogue. The one language of true dialogue is that which reaches a sufficient degree of desacralization to be universally employed. In other words, an authentically human culture which allows men to speak and live together in this age of religious and ideological pluralism can be nothing except secular.

If we return now to our point of departure, must we say that in this domain the only concern of the Church lies in the area of reconciliation? After having stressed the role of the Church as one of fostering dialogue, we must now treat of her responsibility in the work of renewal. If men find themselves threatened by separation because of walls of silence, this condition cannot be attributed only to the gradual disintegration of culture or to a cultural void. Men are also separated from one another by antagonistic cultures and by pseudo-cultures. The need for the desacralization of culture has been noted above. At the present time, human cultures, however, tend to identify themselves with modern religions. This is true insofar as the great traditional religions such as Islam, Hinduism, Buddhism, and sometimes, unfortunately, Christianity, impose their mark on the culture of countries where they predominate. It is true, also, for the pseudo-religious ideologies such as Communism which sacralize culture, imposing on it historical, scientific, and philosophical taboos. It is more critically true in terms of that cultural substratum which is common to nearly all contemporary societies, that is, Western science and technology. We have already examined all that can and must be said regarding the positive aspects of the secularity of the modern world. We can never forget that this quality of secularity proceeds directly from Christianity and constitutes an authentic restoration of the dignity of the world and of the liberty of those men who share in it.

Nevertheless, in an attempt to simplify matters, we run the risk of overlooking the ambiguity of the "secularization" phenomenon. By liberating thought from the ontocratic structures which affirm the sacred character of the world, Christianity has given men the liberty to dominate and exploit nature. Yet this human activity can once again turn against man and enslave him anew. Is not man becoming the slave of that science and technology which in the past as in the present represent a magnificent conquest? This question must at least be asked in view of the burden which material needs represent for mankind. Attention must be given to the deliberate stimulation of these needs and to the methods of psychological manipulation used by states and economic forces. Man today is threatened by a loss of freedom in the very measure that his thought is conditioned from without and his future, stripped bare of its secrets, becomes determined fatality.

Under such conditions, must we become reactionary? Are science and technology to be rejected because of their dangers? Should we strive to rebuild a pre-technical society and culture? This would be absurd. Science and technology are here to stay. They cannot be erased. The Christian's task consists in seeking how to put them to good use. That presupposes the preparation of scholars and technicians who can act responsibly and who, before acting, are concerned about the results of their undertakings. Above all, such a project demands a considerable effort of the imagination and of reflection, especially in the areas of theology and the secular. This effort should be directed toward the elaboration of an ethic and a philosophy which no longer consider as totally incompatible the methods of modern science and that liberty without which man is depersonalized. There is need also for a concept of human liberty which would be no longer strictly personal, as in Western thought, but collective and communitarian, thus revalidating one of the forgotten aspects of biblical revelation. There is need, furthermore, for a philosophy of history which will both denounce the illusions of strict determinism and recognize its explicative value. Statistical projection and prognosis need not be destroyers of liberty, but valuable, necessary elements for understanding a history whose secret lies not in intrinsic complexity but in the eschatological Lordship of Jesus Christ.

It would be impossible to present here the long list of all the questions and criticisms which the Church must formulate in regard to the great contemporary cultural tendencies. What is certain is that she must not withdraw into an ivory tower from which she will legislate for human cultures or promulgate a Christian culture elaborated in a vacuum. Nor must she restrict herself to a more or less joyful sharing in the cultural life of men without attempting to bring any critical evaluation to it, or accept such a cultural conformism that the witness of the Church is reduced to the espousal of human wisdom. The danger is not only theoretical. Our Churches have often built ivory towers and they still often dwell in them. On the other hand, the reality of contemporary theological confusion also gives us many reasons to beware. It might well be feared that, by virtue of wanting to live with men, to be in the world as they are, and to find in the world the signs of God's activity, Christians might become no more than citizens *of* the world, believers in a secular and totally human religion, for whom God, in truth, would be dead.

* * *

In this brief essay, more questions have been asked than answers given. We are living in a period of uncertainty, of challenge in regard to the precise situation of the Church in the world, theological reflection on the world, and Christian ethics concerning the world. It is difficult to situate the problem, for every question that is asked inevitably gives rise to others. More and more clearly we come to see that the challenge is directed toward our concept of the Church and our notion of history. It has often been said that our age is one of "ecumenical reformation." Are we to look upon this great renewal of the Church, in view of rediscovered unity that coincides historically with a profound crisis of our civilization and our Christian ethic, as an added difficulty or as a grace of God? The assessment of values, ideas, and methods and the reorganization of our Churches are certainly overwhelming tasks, humanly speaking. But perhaps the breakdown of so many traditions long held as sacred will give our Churches a priceless opportunity to restore their unity, to find a new ethical standard, and to discover a valid life-style. With new freedom, the Churches can find new ways to express the witness we must give to Jesus Christ, this being the primary task of the Church in regard to the world and the domain in which the most radical revision seems necessary. At any rate, if the work to be done seems humanly overwhelming, our judgment cannot stop at merely human considerations. A human Church would be destined either to failure or to pride. The Church, we may be thankful, is first and foremost the Body of Christ and the community to which the Holy Spirit has been promised.

PART TWO

Transfigured World

NIKOS A. NISSIOTIS

Introduction

It can be stated without hesitation that the subject
under discussion here is one of the most important in
Christian theology. Reasons for an increase of interest
in this subject today come from two quarters. On the
one hand, contemporary theologians, in the Western
world especially, are becoming more aware of the insufficiency of a medieval type of theology which has
not succeeded in mastering the dichotomy between
nature and grace, between the sacred and the profane,
between the divine and the temporal. This failure per-
sists despite a desire to unify the two spheres, ordering
them through subjection of the natural world to the
unique personal revelation in Christ. It is precisely this
subjection which is challenged, insofar as it has been
determined by theories which admit a continuity between a multiform natural theology and a properly
Christian theology, achieved by the imposing effort of
a synthesizing mind. The affirmation that the whole
world is placed under the dominion of the singular
personal revelation of God betrays the unrealistic and
conventional character of such theories.

On the other hand, there is an increasing interest in this subject in proportion to the obvious evolution of the Christian masses toward "secularism" out of what was formerly simply known as the "secular," that is, the exercise of the non-religious, non-ecclesiastical professions. We are thinking here of the movement of emancipation which is perceptible today under extremely varied forms. In affecting a large segment of supposedly Christian populations, this movement extends from a simple claim for independence of life and of thought to radical atheism, from antitheism to militant anticlericalism.

Furthermore, numerous specific questions are being asked and they demand a new theological attitude which cannot be as separatist or as self-sufficient as former attitudes. Indeed, the problem does not present itself only to that part of the Christian world which has subordinated the temporal to the divine or has professed the theory of the "two Kingdoms" because it was nourished on scholastic theology. This is an urgent problem facing all Christians in all continents, reaching beyond confessional divergencies. Wherever the Church seeks to evangelize and proclaim the Word of God, wherever she would act as a Christian community in the modern world, she meets the same questions about her relationship to that world. The problem is a difficult one for the Oriental Churches, too, in spite of a more flexible (because more cosmic) basis of Greek patristic theology and despite the famous Byzantine theory of the "symphony" existing between the divine and the temporal. In countries like Greece, where an effort is made to maintain this symphony, technical civilization challenges the coexistence of state and the Church. The reciprocal relationship of the two is questioned, as is their mutual respect within the framework of a full collaboration between the temporal and the divine. In other countries of the Orthodox tradition in the East, the same technical civilization coincides with the formation of states which declare themselves officially atheistic in severing all connections with the Church. In countries where the majority of the population is Moslem, traditional structures are broken so that the "Church and world" theme presents a thorny question for theologians in those areas too.

In terms of any interconfessional study in which Roman Catholics, representatives of the various Churches of the Reform, and members of the Orthodox tradition are associated, the difficulty is augmented in a twofold manner. On one hand, our notion of the world is confused and vague. On the other, we differ in our concept of the Church. We must, then, undertake a delicate exegetical study of these two terms. In this way, it will be possible to enunciate several fundamental principles which will enable us to study together this essential problem, with a view to shared evangelical action in the contemporary world.

I

THE CONCEPT
OF "WORLD"

CONTEMPORARY literature gives us a vivid picture of the divergence of opinions among theologians on what the "world" represents for them as Christians. The Constitution on the Church in the Modern World of Vatican II is no exception. Indeed, it presents an image of this divergence in its attempt to suggest a synthesis of the most important currents of thought on this subject in Roman Catholicism and in other Churches.

For some, the world seems to be the whole of reality existing outside the Church. This is inconceivable for the Orthodox patristic tradition, according to which the Church is the world transfigured, the primordial "cosmic" reality, the axis of the cosmos understood as this concrete world of ours and not as a universal and supernatural abstraction. Cosmic reality is the reality of this historical world. There is no other word in Greek to signify the world except *cosmos*. (This point will be examined further in our discussion of cosmic ecclesiology.)

For other theologians "the world" designates those tremendous possibilities released through the mediation of the machine between material nature and scientific man under the influence of technical progress. Or again, it might refer to the dynamic aspect of matter in relation to the human intelligence that sets free natural potentialities to assure a continual progress toward man's material well-being. The notion of world is then identified in a certain measure with the evolutionary process of humanity and gives birth to a kind of theological optimism. Such a theory rests on the idea that progress is a gift of God and that the historical Christman provides the dynamic basis of this evolution through his incarnation, which results in the hominization of man. This doctrine, which is extremely widespread today in all Christian confessions, tends to lose sight of the mystery of the Incarnation in its totality. The Incarnation, that is, the act of God assuming human flesh in Christ, reaches beyond Bethlehem to include Golgotha, the Cross, and the Resurrection. Moreover, we must not forget that this total revelation requires a very difficult achievement—the personal metamorphosis of individual man in the Church. The generalized Christology of the "new theology" eliminates by its optimism the specific message of the Gospel as proclaimed by the Christian community to the world. It suppresses that biblical dualism by which the world is perceived as the creation of the love of God but disordered by the rebellious liberty of man.

The new, optimistic Christian monism does not succeed in apprehending the insurmountable dialectic and the implicit discontinuity in those biblical texts which affirm the love of God for the world. "God has so loved the world that he gave his only Son so that every man who believes in him will not perish" (Jn. 3:16). It is true that in the cosmic vision of the early Orthodox

Church a certain kind of generalized Christology and an evangelical optimism were professed. These notions, expressed above all in the writings of the mystical Fathers, held that everything in this world is saved under the Lordship of Christ, as perceived in the transfiguration of Tabor and in the Resurrection. This vision, however, is somewhat different from that which is found today in some theologians. The former was given only by the Spirit of God, like a new revelation developing after Pentecost through the history of the Church. It is necessary, then, to make a distinction between the simple presence of Christ in the world by reason of his Incarnation, which is the unique event that opens up new possibilities of comprehending the world, and that knowledge which man has of Christ through the Spirit within the communion of the Church.

For Christian theology, a just notion of the world and its consequent evaluation does not depend on a simplistic affirmation of the presence of Christ *along with* a human history in full, dynamic evolution. The separation between the Church and the world is not bridged by means of global, general theories which grant the primacy to a positive outlook on this world, which is in a fundamental identity with a perfectly human Christ. Theology, to safeguard the twofold biblical vision of the world, must not only underline this identity but indicate as well the discontinuity between the Gospel and historical reality. It must be recognized, nevertheless, that, methodologically, this new theology renders a precious service to a rigid scholasticism, still enclosed in a limited vision which is focused on itself and its own principles. This optimism reminds us that the world is always there and that no authentic theology, still less an ecclesiology, can be produced without reference to the actual, here-and-now world.

This does not mean that the world is going to dictate the norms by which the nature of the Church is to be interpreted. It does mean that the ecclesial community is not solely a transhistorical or eschatological communion in vertical relation with "its" triune God. The horizontal plane of relation to the world is equally given a priori by God to the Church as the domain of her existence and her action. Ecclesiology is a commentary on the event whereby the people of God are gathered together after their dispersion, to be once again dispersed in and for the world. Pentecost is more than the summons of the people of God to an assembly that is chosen but set aside from this world; it is also a sending-forth into the world—a dynamic, creative relation that reconstitutes the world through the grace of the holy Trinity which has created the universe, maintaining it in love and continually regenerating it.

Thus the life of the Church is inseparable from what is called the world. In an ecclesiological perspective, a vision of the world is attained that is not primarily the result of sociological analysis or of any new understanding of secularization. What matters in this perspective is the composition of the Church, made up of the human community in communion with the personal triune God. The community created by God, a transfigured world bearing all the characteristics of terrestrial life, can never be renounced under pretext of giving priority to the human reality. Such an attitude adds no value to the world but isolates it from a proper and authentic relationship with God in and through his community. It is true that social structures, economic enterprises, and national traditions exert a considerable influence in the formation and transformation of the structures of the Church. It is essential to keep these factors in mind in the work of renewing the Church.

Such considerations, however, are not of primary importance in the way the Christian Church looks at the world.

Life and the world, as we contemplate them through the human person, show forth in depth the unbreakable relation between God and man manifested by the simple existence of the Christian community at the heart of this world. If the Church is to be defined in terms of the world and in conjunction with it, there is no question of purely and simply replacing ecclesiology by Christian sociology. Rather, an authentic cosmology must be made out of ecclesiology, through situating the "world" as it is seen through the Church, as a totality potentially redeemed in Christ.

Against this background, it is clear that the Orthodox tradition does not have a vision of the world which is modified in each era according to the development of technical progress or of new sociological structures. It is neither pessimistic nor optimistic in regard to contemporary ideologies. In its eyes, the technological age has not given birth to a new man, qualitatively different from the man of former, outmoded eras. Before the Word of God and its historical community, the Church, the world presents itself continually, under all its forms, as on-the-way toward conversion, as moving from false autonomy to theonomy, from profane independence to the freedom of the ecclesial communion.

Every vision and every interpretation of the world in the Orthodox tradition operates on the basis of this dialectic. The world is the supreme gift which God makes to us, one of a community restored through and in the Church. It is fallen humanity which must pass from anthropocentrism to theocentrism by means of personal repentance. Yet, today, the world is in the process of creating a new humanism founded on the self-sufficiency of human progress and technology.

Under these circumstances, secularism must not be studied only as an indirect result of biblical influence. It is indispensable that we see another, deeper aspect of secularism today. We must see man in his own autonomy, freed from all dependence on a personal God. The theological vision of the modern secularized world must include the negative aspect of this secularization in relation to the Gospel. That is, we must recognize the absolute value which secularism attributes not only to material objects and to technology, but, analogically, to humanity itself and to man's evolutionary progress, giving no consideration to any other finality or teleology of human life beyond this progress.

This secularized notion of the world is also characterized by an activism which attempts to grasp the domain of the secular through a purely functional perspective. Today antimetaphysical tendencies often result from a concept of the world which denies its substance as a divine-human communion. While positivistic pragmatism is necessary and legitimate in the sciences, it becomes catastrophic if it leads to a mechanical solipsism that cuts off introspection and reflection in depth. A notion of the world which is abstracted from its origin and from its transcendental end runs the risk of maintaining a superficial, overly optimistic view of technical progress and of confounding material progress with spiritual growth and development.

These are the real problems which involve our ecclesiology in a difficult dialogue not with the world—for there is no object "world" outside the Church—but with the simplistic concepts of certain contemporary theologians. Without any question, full credit must be accorded technical progress and the evolution of mankind. At the same time, our ecclesiology of the Church-world relation must undertake a study of the new humanism. It must examine this new autonomy which has gone beyond humanization in the image of Christ to an antitheistic, antireflective movement which deprives the human person of his basic qualities. To be studied also is the phenomenon of automation, which involves modern man in psychic difficulties at the moment when he ought to participate in the sociological structures which are giving new shapes to human social life. We are no longer faced with the radical emancipated individualism of the materialists or rationalists. It is now a question of an emancipation of man in general, as he aspires to the formation of an autonomous universal family without regard to his origins or the end of his life, without consideration of the world insofar as it is an immediate, experienced reality. We are faced by an intrasubjectivity in which the value of the thinking, acting subject is measured by his fidelity to the self-sufficiency of a technocratic humanity and its goal of a universal progress that unites all subjects in a noble common effort for the well-being of the entire world.

In this situation, the supreme task of Christian theology is the construction of truly biblical ecclesiologies. This must be accomplished before undertaking the analysis of the special problems which are presented under the title of "Church and world." It must be achieved while deliberately avoiding every unilateral approach, whether in favor of the world or the Church. The unity of the divine with the human must be preserved in and through the reality of the Christian community. This unity must suffer no modification, no fusion of the two elements which would eliminate the distinction between God and man. In fact, the kind of theory we have been discussing, by advocating an identity of these two realms, would introduce the contrary of what it aims to establish. Its conclusion would be a separation of the Church and the world, effected by the world.

A balanced ecclesiology seeks to avoid deviations toward extreme, unilateral positions through attention to two essential points: an ecclesiological cosmology and a pneumatological Christian anthropology. These two points furnish the basis for a study of the relationship between the Church and the world in the light of well-defined ideas. They concentrate in the first place on the nature of the Church in regard to the world and then on the worth of the human person, one of the major scriptural values and the fundamental constitutive element of this world and of the Church. Nevertheless, it is not possible to enter immediately into a consideration of these two points without clarifying also the notion of Church. The detour is indispensable for this study, since our present ecclesiologies are often influenced by confessional polemics, especially in the West by reason of the Reformation. From the beginnings of Church history there was a difference of ecclesiological concepts between the East and the West, and this finally resulted in the schism of 1054. Today, frequent misunderstandings between Western and Eastern theologians on the question of the relation of the Church to the world proceed from different interpretations of the Church. It cannot be denied that the rigorous organization and institutionalization of the Roman Church, along with her activism (the same applies to the evangelical Churches), conceals a conception of the Church which is very unlike that meant by the Orthodox East when she speaks of *ecclesia*. This difference and a proper appreciation of it seem most important for a common study of the Church-world problem in an authentically ecumenical perspective.

These two modes of treating ecclesiology are not incompatible. On the contrary, they are to a certain degree complementary; using them, we may arrive at an ecclesiology which will reflect more universally the nature of the mystery of the Church as it can be discerned in the biblical text and as her members have lived it throughout history and are still living it today.

"CHURCH" IN RELATION TO "WORLD"

PRESENT ecumenical relations have considerably favored ecclesiological studies and have thrown much light onto the confusion reigning over this subject by reason of the separation between Christian communities. Two positions are becoming increasingly clarified due to the ecclesiological discussions between Christians of separate traditions and especially because of personal contacts, direct and reciprocal participation in the life of other Churches, and prayer in common. This development of a community life among the different Churches is slowly unveiling the sources of differences, the initial causes of varying interpretations of the nature of the Church, and the different attitudes of Christian communities in regard to the world today.

This last point is of special interest for the present study. As the result of direct contact between separated Christians, comparative theology (*Konfessionskunde*), in which a professor ordinarily enumerates the ecclesiological differences of other confessions (seen from without), has become almost outdated by events. To-day, there is a tendency to know the other communi-ties of the one, indivisible Church by sharing their life from within.

The following pages are written in this spirit, even though some of the phrases employed may give the impression of being basically a criticism of certain Western positions and a defense of the Eastern tradi-tion. Our aim is to seek greater light in ecclesiology, to foster discussion among the different traditions in hope of their collaboration in the world.

When the Christian communities of the West and of the East are known directly, with their political and religious histories, their philosophical and cultural bases, and the milieus in which these different commu-nities have been created and developed, it becomes clear that their ecclesiologies are the result of a refer-ence not only to divine revelation but also to the sur-rounding world. In the West, the Church had to inter-pret the phenomenon of the "Church" on the basis of juridical order and thought. Above all, she had either to replace the Roman state, which was in its decadence in certain countries of the West after the first half of the third century, or to establish new states among the non-civilized European peoples. In both cases, the Church had to furnish at the outset the foundations of faith and the structure of a state, with all the details necessary for community and national life. Placed in such cir-cumstances, the Church was burdened, interiorly, with a rigorous monarchical system while, exteriorly, she was caught up in social and political activism. The result of this double phenomenon was a unification of the religious and the political powers, with primacy given to the former.

Active participation in all the affairs of the world and the internal organization of the Church gradually created, in the West, a form of ecclesiastical life and thought which focused on sociological realities. This made the Church a well-ordered organism, acting visibly and explicitly on principles favoring the unification of the two powers. The Church appeared to be then, principally, an institution and, as such, one superior to all other human institutions, even though she bore the same characteristics as they. Without losing sight of her sacramental and transcendental essence, the Latin Church nevertheless strongly underlined her institutional and sociological character.

This attitude has generally been highly criticized by the Orthodox. Today, it is looked upon rather as the result of an historical evolution which is comprehensible as far as the reasons which provoked it are concerned. It is to be condemned in the subsequent exaggerations to which it inevitably led. Nevertheless, these exaggerations have not succeeded in substantially altering the Church's proper character which consists in being the site and the instrument of redemptive grace. The following principles of the Roman position can be briefly presented as being of special interest for our study.

1. The world is to be reorganized in all its details on the new foundation given by God: the redemption of all men. All men are to conform their personal and public lives absolutely and totally to the truth. The salvation transmitted by the Church to men is not destined uniquely to transform the individual believer in the Church, insofar as he is a member of the Body of Christ; it does, however, imply a new order, a new justice, a renewed organization of the entire world. The Church possesses the principles by which the world can be reordered, by which all its problems can be solved. The Church does not teach a merely personal code of ethics, but one also meant to be public. She can pro-

nounce on all social and family problems through
reference to the divine law, which is expressed through
her with the supreme authority of its own divine right.

2. This divine right is the characteristic which dis-
tinguishes the Church among all other institutions of
the world and, thanks to this gift of God, gives the
Church a place above any other authority on earth.
The superiority of the ecclesiastical institution is juridical as well as pastoral. Not only does the Church judge
all institutions which are not vested, as she is, with
divine authority, but she gives to all other institutions
their foundation and their spiritual nourishment. The
Church is not opposed to institutions which maintain
the order of creation, since the same God created this
order and sent Christ to man, but she does judge and
condemn any deviations in them. Both the distinction
between the sacred and the profane and their identity
rest on this truth.

Under the authority of the ecclesiastical institution,
everything in the world is gathered into a single, universal family. The catholicity of the Church is not only
the plenitude of the truth of Christ lived and manifested in the local Churches throughout the world, it
is also one organism, structured from its summit down,
united under a single authority at once juridical and
pastoral, visible and personified. For the Catholic
Church, the presence of this authority is manifested not
only wherever a bishop resides at the heart of a local
community; nor is union translated only by means of
a national synod. There must be a manifestation of
union stemming from a universal center and a universal bishop in whom are united all power and all authority. Bishops do not constitute pastoral authority unless
they are all united together in collegiality with their
leader, their head. The pope is not simply a local
bishop; his place, central in the apostolic see, consti-

tutes him universal bishop, invested by reason of this
office with all power on earth.

For the Orthodox tradition, there is a deviation or
an exaggeration here, which has developed as a result
of a situation which was justifiable in the beginning
when the dynamic presence of the Church was necessary for the world. The danger in this deviation lies in
the universalism of its ecclesiology. This would form
Christianity around a juridical center into something
which threatens to give the appearance of a sacred
totality facing the world. Such an attitude was adopted
and applied with good reason in the West in the course
of the first centuries of the Christian era and during the
Middle Ages. It permitted an effective union of the
sacred and the profane while safeguarding the primacy
of the former. Uultimately, it became a source of radical separation among Christians and of opposition between the Church and the world. Finally, it provoked
internal rupture, since some parties in the Church
could not accept this universalized ecclesiology. On one
hand, the primacy of love, granted according to ancient
tradition to the first apostolic see, the see of Rome,
became primacy of jurisdiction. On the other hand, the
function of Peter, seen under its juridical aspect, becomes absolutely identified with that of the bishop of
Rome. These facts constitute an evolution for which
Orthodoxy finds no justification either in the Bible or
in the life of the Church during the first ten centuries.
It is encouraging to see that Vatican Council II showed
a great effort to reflect upon this point, first of all in
its ecclesiology, and then, as a logical consequence, in
the Constitution on the Church in the Modern World.

3. Thus the Church in the West has placed strong
emphasis on her visibility and her immediate presence.
Her sincere intention was to serve the world by all the
means at her disposition through participation in all

aspects of its life: social, economic, political. The result, however, has been at times to relegate to a secondary plane her role as a sacramental, charismatic community; not primarily to assure the service of sacrament and Word, but to establish a sacred order which will unify the world under her authority. It must not be said that the Roman Church has totally neglected her sacramental role. The juridical aspect of her ecclesiology and her individualistic universalism have, however, undermined the full import of certain biblical principles. These factors have also diminished her interest in the preservation of the unity of the Church, in a mission and a task pursued on all levels without concern for a universal central authority.

Thus the Church of Rome gives the impression of not having maintained a balance between the divine and the human in her ecclesiology. She gives this impression in spite of her religious and missionary activity, the extraordinary labors of her religious orders, the overwhelming sacrifices of her devoted faithful, and her astonishing liturgical and theological vitality. She gives this impression at least to the Eastern Churches where, it must be admitted, some of these very signs of vitality are absent.

Many things have contributed to lack of balance just mentioned. Among them are the human aspects of the institution, the absolute identity of apostolicity and catholicity with the hierarchy, and above all the position accorded to the vicar of Christ, invested with the full power of authority. The argument from divine right cannot even begin to save an ecclesiology which calls into question the union of the two principles of the Church's existence, namely, the divine and the human, in the image of the two natures of Christ. One has the impression that even if, in Latin ecclesiology, priority is granted to the divine (as shown by its respect for the sacramental, liturgical, and monastic life), real priority seems finally to be given to the human. This is so because the Church professes identity with Christ as an ecclesiastical institution, particularly in terms of her hierarchy and above all else in her visible head on this earth. Historicity, human reality, and the immediate realization of the divine economy have shaken and upset the mystical, the charismatic, the theophanic.

In conformity with this evolution, the Roman Church attempts to interpret to the world and to all terrestrial realities the real presence of Christ, Savior and unique Lord. This presence must be immediately given by the Church through identification with its own forms. It must be preached or professed in all the domains of daily life, with conviction, as an absolute truth in and for this world. Latin ecclesiology since the Middle Ages is marked by a sort of absolute certitude regarding the Christological basis of the Church as total identification with the presence of the Church militant in the world. The negation of human liberty, the sin of man, the opposition of evil to the Lordship of Christ: none of these facts provoked any hesitation in the thought of the Church. The triumph of the risen Christ immediately becomes a permanent presence of the triumph of the Church.

This is an attitude which Orthodoxy affirms emphatically, but with an entirely different meaning. The difference in the two traditions is highly important here. This difference rests on the fact that, for the Orthodox, Christ is present in the world through and in the Holy Spirit and by the mediation of the eucharistic community and the proclaimed word. The Christological basis of the Church is neither conceived nor applied aside from a pneumatology flowing logically from a truly trinitarian theology. The Christology of Rome often gives the impression of having overlooked the fact that

the presence of Christ is effected by the Spirit. This
permits an immediate identification of Christ with
forms and institutions, and defines the lordship of
Christ as being *in via* toward its eschatological pleroma.
The Christology of Rome also overlooks the value of
the ecclesial community formed by the members of the
Church who, qualitatively, insofar as they are spirit-
bearing, are absolutely equal. Sacerdotal and charismatic distinctions can certainly be established among
those who are members of the Body of Christ through
the Spirit. What can never be admitted is the absolute
identity of one or several of these members with Christ,
with a particular Apostle, or with the Eleven. Continuity must not become ontological identity.

Thus the concept of the Church in Latin theology
betrays anthropocentrism in its identity theories and in
its practice. It is true that this anthropocentrism helps
greatly to root the Church in the world, to foster its
activity, to render it more present to daily life and its
problems. Working in this way, however—which might
in general be an admirable way to work—the Church
is always tempted to concern herself with too much, to
give general or particular answers to all the questions
asked by the world, and at times to humanize the
kerygma just a little too much. In the last analysis, the
concept of the juridical priority of the Church intro-
duces a pan-ecclesiasticism which humanizes divine
grace and runs the risk of provoking from the world
violent reactions and radical anticlericalism.

It would be absurd to try to sketch for Protestant
theology a single image of the Church in regard to the
world. Neither the circumstances under which the
Reformation was produced nor the varying form and
development of the evangelical Churches permit facile
generalizations. What can be said is that the Reformers
wanted to reject the human aspect of the Church, the

institution which had been absolutized on the basis of divine right and sacred monarchy according to the theory of the immediate and personified representation of Christ in the world. Through lack of direct contact between the two great divisions of Christianity, the Eastern Church had been able to ignore what transpired at Rome. The East began to repulse this development only when Rome attempted in the practical order to extend her principles and her universalistic institution into the Eastern world.

The Protestant Churches, as offspring of the Latin Church, bear in themselves the same spiritual tradition and the same habits of thought. In wishing to correct Roman deviations, the Protestant Churches, through force of circumstances, felt they had to separate from the Roman Church and revolted against her. Orthodoxy, on the contrary, had from the beginning followed its own way without ever adhering to the doctrine and practice of Rome as these clearly and explicitly developed after the eighth century. The effort of the Reform to reestablish the equilibrium between the divine and human was absolutely legitimate. So too was its effort to free the ecclesiastical institution from false identification between its head and the divinely-given authority of Peter. The Reformation was intended to reestablish the pneumatological basis by which a juridical Christianity would be overcome. It was intended above all to diminish the clericalism and the excessive authority of the hierarchy of the time.

Nevertheless, the fact that the Reform took place at the heart of Roman Catholicism forced it to be primarily an independence movement. It necessarily had to overlook the importance of the ecclesiastical communion since it had to free itself from the domination of principles it judged to be false. Obviously, in this context, the Holy Spirit would be looked upon first of all as the supreme gift of God bringing about freedom from the Roman institution and then from every ecclesiastical institution. The weakness of the theology of the Holy Spirit in medieval ecclesiology prevented the Reform from grasping the full significance of an ecclesiological pneumatology before it went on to speak of the personal sanctification of each believer in the Christian community. Thus, for the Reform, the Holy Spirit, the divine gift, served to place redeemed man beyond every institution. This can be clearly perceived in the development of new Churches following the Reformation. These groups looked upon the fixed and unchangeable forms of the Church as no better than functional necessities, and sought an emancipation that was certainly communitarian but whose pneumatological inspiration remained personal rather than ecclesial.

In rejecting the monarchical hierarchy of the Latin Church founded on divine right, certain of the later Reformation Churches were not able to recognize that the ecclesial institution was established by the work of the Holy Spirit on Pentecost. The institution of the Church is charismatic. While it possesses some characteristics common to human institutions, it is distinguished from them because it is animated by divine love and not by human rights, laws, and categories. The Church exists as a fixed, visible institution invested in its fundamental forms with an absolute value for the whole Church and for all ages. These forms are transparent and flexible. They reform themselves each time those administering them act in accordance with the love infused by the Paraclete when the Church was constituted an institution to render pastoral service, the burden of every ecclesial community.

Instead of elaborating an ecclesial pneumatology, the Reform replaced divine right by another principle, scriptural and correct to begin with but growing into new deviations through later absolutization and unilateral application. This principle is the theology of the Word of God which, after the Reform, held exactly the same place as that attributed to the work of the Paraclete for the Orthodox. It is the Word which judges the Church, which effects her reform, which incorporates ecclesiastical institutions into a process of permanent transformation. By this fact the Church, which is the center and the community of the Spirit, finds herself under the abstract judgment of the Word; the Word becomes the judge of the Church which bears the Word of salvation and regeneration, which produces the holy books of the Bible, and which alone has the right to canonize them.

Actually, the Scriptures and the sacramental, existential life of the Church belong to and share each other in the single event of salvation. Word, institution, sacraments, mission—all are one in an inseparable union. No one element can judge the whole. The priority of the Word and proclamation over the other constitutive elements of the Church has become in the majority of the Reform Churches the very foundation of the Church and the element which judges her in every instance.

We are faced here with a reversal by which the primary constitutive element of the Church takes the place of her true founder and permanent judge. In the last analysis, the Church runs the risk of being nothing other than the assembly of men, judged as sinful and criticized on all sides by those who interpret and preach the Word of God as private individuals. We know the judgment pronounced against the seven local Churches of Asia Minor in the Apocalypse. We forget that it is precisely not the Word of God so much as skilful exegesis which judges these few (not all) Churches of Asia Minor. It is the Holy Spirit who reminds the Churches what the Spirit has said to them individually at each moment of their historical life.

If the Church is to be judged at all, it is to be by the

Spirit, who will express judgment through the voice of
one group of the faithful or one individual, but in any
case through members of the one, holy, catholic, and
apostolic Church. The Church reaches far beyond the
Bible in her preaching and her sacraments. She exists
in history as the accomplishment of the saving work of
Christ through the work of the Holy Spirit who makes
this salvation an historical reality par excellence.

In the eyes of the Orthodox Church, the Reform has
clearly stayed at an anthropocentric level, insisting on
the sociological aspect rather than on the transcendental mystery of the Church. Actually, some extreme
forms of Protestantism assume a radical position and
employ the word "Church" only in the sense of a human assembly and institution. In the spirit of our times,
which rejects every institutional structure in the name
of human liberty, this ecclesiology proclaims the
superiority of man the believer over the ecclesiastical
institution. Such a proclamation concludes that the
Church, in her encounter with the secularization of the
modern world, must abandon all affirmation of the
transhistorical event which she represents and every
reference to her system and her sacramental life, so as
to speak more directly to the world of today.

In order to remain present to modern society,
in this view, she must no longer preach the Word of
God as a summons to men to be transformed in the
Church, but must become secularized herself. Christ,
it is asserted, is not only present in the Word and the
sacrament offered by the Church as a community distinct from this world, he is present in society in its
dynamic progress toward perfection as human community in the image of the Christ-man. The Church does
not sanctify man and life by means properly reserved
to her. In the image of Christ, the Church is called to
sacrifice herself. Christ created true community life for

men by recreating and perfecting the humanity of men through the affirmation of their mutual and dynamic interdependence. The Church must sacrifice herself as an institution in an attempt to conform to this human reality which infinitely surpasses her in the new humanity of modern societies.

According to this modern theology, professed by some Protestants, Christ is immediately present wherever there is revolution for the well-being of human society. He is present where a gigantic work is underway to foster the progress of man as member of the new society. He is more present in such places than in the Church through the repetition of traditional preaching and the sacraments. Liturgy must be more than a repetition of outmoded forms irrelevant in the light of the event of modern society. True liturgy is the work of this society as society; it is the consciousness of each member of the society that his work is a service of man in horizontal communion with other men with whom he is in solidarity and for whom he is responsible.

This attitude manifests a strictly anthropocentric ecclesiology and an optimistic, abstract interpretation of the modern world. It certainly does not transmit the general evangelical point of view. It cannot be considered as the dominant Protestant position today. What is interesting, in spite of all else, is to see in this extreme position the extension of an anthropocentric ecclesiology to its limits on the basis of the humanity of Christ, without allusion to the work of the Holy Spirit. But it is the Spirit who summons the Church as a sanctified and separate community into the world, and it is this work of the Spirit which thus presupposes a pneumatological ecclesiology.

The "social gospel" and the unilateral exaggerations to which it gave birth looked upon the philanthropic social work of the Church as the only mode of her presence in the world. In the same way, this new, uniquely anthropocentric theology makes the Church a purely human institution existing only through and for the world. It thus threatens to compromise the specific message of the Gospel which is an ever-renewed call to the world from a personal, triune God. This prophetic message is lost through a secularized ecclesiology. Lost too, are the means of sanctification which, as gifts of grace from the Holy Spirit, remain identical and unchangeable throughout the centuries in their meaning and in their fundamental traits. Such an ecclesiology gradually leads to a loss of the meaning of the Body of Christ. The Church is rendered void of her content, that is, trinitarian grace and spiritual, sacramental, charismatic life. She becomes a center of humanitarian action or an association of optimistic intellectuals who attribute to the modern world entirely too positive a value.

III

ECCLESIOLOGICAL COSMOLOGY
AND THE WORLD

CURRENT ecclesiologies are most interesting in that they cast light on theology's search today to find meaning for "Church and world." To avoid all misunderstanding, the first question to ask theologians of the different confessions who are engaged in this study is their meaning of the Church. Many phrases which are mutually shocking to theologians are the fruit of an ecclesiology which is not shared by all and which determines greatly different principles and postures on the subject of the Church in the world.

THE CHURCH IN THE WORLD

Confronted by these principles and by the evolution of Western ecclesiology, the Orthodox Church presents an attitude founded on a theocentric ecclesiology in regard to the world. Orthodoxy declares that the community of the Church is the work of the Holy Spirit by virtue of the redemptive work of Christ. This is the proclamation of an absolute affirmation without support from any theory of divine right expressed through a monarchically structured magisterium. The Church is the communion of saints. Her holiness is due not to the holiness of men but to the continual work of the Paraclete who creates, constitutes, and perfects her as Church. The primacy of the divine over the human is translated for Orthodox ecclesiology in the words of the Nicene Creed, which declares that the Church is holy and thus she can never be called sinful, even though she is made up of men who are sinners. Absolute priority is given to the divine work of permanent sanctification accomplished by the Holy Spirit who unites the holy head with the body of sinner-members in order to purify them and to regenerate them through the gifts of grace. The origin and the end of the Church are indisputably found in the work of the Holy Trinity. The full and immediate triune revelation effects the participation of man even now in the perfect divine-human community, promised for the end of time. The purely human assembly, or the institution made sacred by divine right, is nothing but an external appearance of the fundamental reality of the Church. The reality consists in allowing the Trinity to accomplish its work and to manifest its power through the Spirit in and through the entire world in every age.

This theocentric ecclesiology affirms a relation between the Church and the world quite different from what we have seen thus far. Certainly, the Church is before all else and preeminently *in, with* and *for* the world. As Church, however, she is not of this world and she is to give the world a theonomous finality. The origin and the end of the Church lie outside the Church, in the initiative of God, in his work and the goal he has assigned her. He has sent her and led her into this world to be the instrument of the ultimate communion of the world in its totality with its Creator. That is why the existence of the Church finds its source in an historical event which, however, does not bestow upon her a proper ontology. Her essence is divine grace through the work of the Paraclete. The institutions of the Church are the expression of this absolutely transcendental, theonomous, divine essence, different from anything which characterizes other human institutions.

These ecclesial institutions function with flexibility and are personified in the communion of the faithful rather than in any hierarchical juridical power. Nevertheless, this community of the faithful is theocratic, not lay, in its direction. All its members are called to a sanctity that is incarnated especially in those charismatic persons who are charged with a service, with a distinct personal diaconate, making them instruments of the transmission of divine grace. The charism of highest value which the Holy Spirit gives to the Church is its institutional aspect. This is the freedom of communion as opposed to the liberty of emancipation found in secular humanism. The institution expresses the order of divine trinitarian love which can be neither broken nor divided. It is the manifestation of perfect pneumatic order. It is the revelation of the power of the Holy Spirit gathering into the creative moving power of the world, into love, all peoples of all times in a single communion on this earth.

By reason of her existence, the Church is the sign that all of humanity is caught up in a dynamic movement of reconciliation with God and with the community. The Church "in the world" means not only that the world becomes the locus of the presence of Christ in his identification with earthly realities in general. It means also that trinitarian grace penetrates all human structures at every moment in a personal and distinct fashion, causing the world to pass from solipsism and anthropocentric autonomy to theonomy and divine-human communion.

Eastern ecclesiology seems at first sight to separate

the world from the event of the Church by reason of an insistence on the holiness of the Church and on her transcendental and theocentric character. This is the tradition, however, which best avoids the dualism between eternal and temporal, divine and human, sacred and profane. Furthermore, Orthodoxy has always insisted on the historicity of the Church and on the value of her terrestrial existence. It has always emphasized in a most concrete manner her cosmic, localized reality experienced as a divine-human community in the *hic et nunc*. The distinction between holiness, the gift of grace of the Holy Spirit made to all men through the Church, and man the sinner, who would appropriate this gift to himself, is not sufficient reason to establish in a vague and abstract way a separation between the Church and the world.

Supported by the Holy Spirit, the creator of communion, the Church cannot be conceived of independently of this world. In fact, the Spirit does not found an otherworldly reality. The Paraclete perfects the Father's creation by virtue of the Son's redemptive action. In the reality of the Church we find a continuity of fulfillment. It moves from creation toward the perfection of the cosmos and of humanity, focusing them in Christ, giving to God in liberty a profoundly dialectical response. The Holy Spirit is not a new God who creates a group of *illuminati* to separate them from the world by inspiring them to lead an exaggerated life in radical opposition to the world. The Holy Spirit is the Paraclete, the Spirit sent by Christ into time, just as Christ had been sent by the Father. After Christ, the Holy Spirit continues the work of salvation by giving to men all that comes from the Father, who unites all in himself (Jn. 16:14, 15).

The creation and the salvation of the world imply a permanent quality in God's relation with the world.

This lasting note has been incarnated by the unique revelation in Christ and by the Church, led by the Spirit in the world. Thus, Christology and pneumatology are the two commentaries on the continual event by which the Church reconstitutes the totality of the world by restoring its original relation as creation of God. Christology refers to the being of God acting personally in his world. Pneumatology speaks of the lasting community of God in this world through his people, the Church. The Church, then, is in the world by virtue of the world's origin, function, and end as defined in the revealing act of the triune God. To say *in* the world means preeminently, inseparably, profoundly, and entirely *in solidarity with the world*. This solidarity is not simply ethical and social. It is essential and organic.

The Church is the world: the world gathered together anew in a single family because of a reestablished, renewed communion with its personal God. The Church is the world as we behold it in the fullness of its humanity, transformed and enlightened by the Word who calls to repentance. This summons enables man to break out of his solitude, his false independence, and move forward to his ultimate goal, which is to be the object of God's perfect love and to live in the common, mutual love of all men. The Church and the world belong mutually to each other, not because of any decision of the clergy or by reason of theories of systematic theology. This truth is given in the original act of the Creator, in the one sacrifice of Christ, and through the work of the Spirit in the entire world at the moment when the Church was founded. That is why Christ is seen in the New Testament as the fulfillment of all creation. Finally, it can be added that the world is *potentially* the Church, for without her the world's existence has no meaning. The Church is the center, the axis, the essence of the world. By the Church, the

world is en route toward its final realization: divine-
human communion. By her existence at the heart of the
world, inseparably united to this world, the Church
constantly proclaims this goal.

Orthodoxy is unable to speak of the intimate relation
between the Church and the world, and to maintain
the distinction between saint and sinner in a personal
and concrete manner, without a cosmic ecclesiology.
This ecclesiology considers the Church at one and the
same time as microcosm and macrocosm. This view
is completely in conformity with the full range of scriptural revelation: creation, incarnation, redemption, regeneration. In this ecclesial community gathered together around the Eucharist and the Word of God, all
of creation is recapitulated and reconstituted. The
totality of the creative work of God and the totality of
the reality of the world are united in an encounter without confusion, in a complete communion, in view of
the end of the world and of time. Thus is realized the
plenitude of the *perichoresis* in which all humanity
shares in the experience of creation, salvation, and
sanctification by the faith-decision to be a part of this
ultimate reality. As microcosm, the Church realizes in
advance the truth of this reality and with complete certainty opens our eyes to this cosmic goal. The role of
the Church is to be even now the occasion, the place
of the world's participation in this event. By anticipation, the sharing is complete.

The Church is at the service of this world. She pre-
figures its ultimate transformation and manifests it here
and now in a manner that is considered anachronistic
and laughable by the world's standards. Her glorified
life is hidden by earthly suffering and human weakness,
thus setting into relief the character of the humiliation
of God's revelation in Christ. The Church has no proper
existence of herself. She exists in and for the world and

she will disappear when complete communion is achieved. She possesses no brilliant wisdom which makes her capable of gaining the world's assent as it stands plunged in its problems. She has no universal, general, easy solutions or answers for these problems. Her solutions are hidden in the souls of individual, concrete men and in their existential anguish. As a microcosm of all creation, the Church of martyrs and of existential witness is perhaps more immediately present to the world than the Church ready to demonstrate her total solidarity with the world by words, answers, and solutions which she proposes. The thirst for proofs of solidarity which is found in an exaggerated activism in the world goes against its affirmed intention. It proves that the Church is separated from the world by her wealth, her rights, her power, by her wisdom and her intelligence. It proves that the Church attempts to reestablish union with the world and to manifest her interest in it by these same means and methods.

There should be no misunderstanding here. The Church need not become a martyr in order to be the Church in the world. She need not keep silent and withhold interest from the actual problems of the world. She need not refuse to act in given, particular situations. Orthodox Christians must be careful not to fall into this error when they criticize the positions of other Christian traditions. When we insist on the theocentrism of the Church, on the cosmic ecclesiology and mutual "belonging" of the Church and the world as so many divinely established facts, we run the risk of falling into a mystical passivity. We have been a little too certain that the reality of our position has enabled us to be both transcendental and fully historical. This attitude, which was correct in the beginning, has created in us and still often creates a sort of sacred hypnosis, a beatific narcosis worse than any social activism set up

as the supreme goal of the presence of the Church in
the world. Ecclesiological cosmology is not only a magnificent speculation, a vision, a conviction. It is the
introduction to the dynamic and real presence of the
Church in the world, through the service of the prophetic word of God in this world.

Social activism, intellectual self-sufficiency, the appeal to divine right, and an optimistic view of secularism appear today as dangerous positions in their
extreme forms. Orthodox Christians must nevertheless
take care that their ecclesiological positions in regard
to the world do not lead them to neglect the prophetic
Word and forget the urgency of action in given, concrete situations. If we withdraw from the world and
unconsciously, without willing it and contrary to our
fundamental Orthodox ecclesiology, isolate ourselves
in a community apart, we betray the true meaning of
our theology of the Church. For this reason and in order
the better to express the Orthodox tradition, another of
its aspects must now be evoked.

THE WORLD IN THE CHURCH

Reciprocal "belonging" as it has been discussed in the
preceding chapter does not consist solely in a unilateral movement on the part of the Church toward
the world. Certainly, the divine act and the continual
work of sanctification of the world by the Church
obliges us to recognize the qualitative priority of the
penetration of the event of the Church in the world.
However, this reality must not lead us to forget, indeed it should remind us, that if this "belonging" is
truly mutual and reciprocal the movement in the opposite direction must also be acknowledged. We must
examine the world in the Church.

It is not possible to construct an ecclesiology regarding the relation of the Church with the world without

speaking of the presence of the world in the Church. Ecclesiological cosmology and the vision of the Church as it is *pars pro toto,* transfigured world and new creation, must not cause us to emphasize only the divine aspect of the Church. In fact, the Church as the Body of Christ is formed by the people of God, that is, by human beings. The world is present in the Church by her members and by her historical reality. If Orthodox Christians insist on the priority and the supremacy of the sanctifying work of the Paraclete and therefore remain intransigent in the face of every ecclesiology which qualifies the Church as sinful, this does not mean that they overlook the terrestrial, human realities of the Church in the world. To say that the Church is holy implies two facts. The Church is sanctified (1) by her union with her head, Christ, through the sanctifying work of the Paraclete and (2) by the sanctification of her members realized by this same Paraclete. This double operation of the Spirit takes place in the world and for the whole world. The union effected is not merely a vertical, Christ-Church relation. Through the humanity of Christ and through the Spirit, it is also horizontal. If the Church cannot be isolated from the world, it is because the world dwells in her through the sinful nature of man, even though this nature is continually sanctified in the Church in the image of the sanctified nature of Christ.

Comprehended in all its depth, the sanctifying work of the Holy Spirit transcends the world, effects the union of Christ with his Body, and unites the world in the Church. This same work reveals the judgment of God in the Church and in the world. The Holy Spirit judges the local Churches in the world because they neglect to proclaim the prophetic word of God. This same work of the Spirit, on which Orthodox Christians take their stand when they insist on the

purity and the holiness of the Church, places in bold
relief the dialectic of the reciprocal belonging that exists
between the Church and the world. The divine-human
communion achieved by the Spirit in the world reveals
not only the glory of grace which triumphs over all evil
on earth, but also reveals the absolute supremacy of
the divine over the human, bringing to light both the
persistence of evil in the Church and her *worldliness*.

The hypostatic union of the two natures of Christ in
a single person, holy and pure, when seen through
ecclesiological cosmology enables us to recognize its
analogy in the divine-human character of the Church
in the world. The confession of faith repeats with strong
conviction that the Church is holy. At the same time,
she needs always to be made holy by the Holy Spirit.
She is subject to his judgment, which renews and sanctifies her. This recalls the fundamental doctrine of
Orthodox Christology concerning the reciprocal but
distinct belonging of the divine and the human. Even
though the divine priority must always be absolutely
respected, this does not mean that the divine is imposed
in an absolute manner on the human or, still less, the
human on the divine. If all is created by the love of the
trinitarian God, through and for his communion, everything is equally marked by human liberty confronted by
the act of love which has created it. Divine love is revealed in its highest degree by the liberty granted to the
human. This freedom is the dynamic sign of divine
creation in love. It animates the history of humanity
and bestows upon man, in the highest manifestation of
his dialectical grandeur, the strength to be free in the
presence of his Creator. This liberty exists also in the
Church, in a kind of passage from emancipation to communion. Man moves from independence to reincorpo-
ration into the divine-human Body.

The liberty of humanity is ever present dialectically in the Church. This liberty establishes communion but can at the same time disrupt it. It is the manifestation of love, but it is also the cause of continual misunderstandings at the heart of the Church, among her own members, when it resists divine grace. The Church is holy and pure. As such, she remains dependent on the judgment of the Spirit. She is holy because she is the spouse of Christ in faith and in the light of the ultimate, eschatological accomplishment of marriage with her Lord who is to come at the end of the ages. Even when the dialectic of human liberty is transformed into divine-human communion in the Church, it can be perceived as the voice of the emancipated world, the world on the march toward its transfiguration in the Church. The ultimate, eschatological marriage is the highest certitude of the historical life of the Church. She is given to us by the *arrabon,* the espousals of the Spirit in the present historical temporality of the Church.

If we see the world through its transfigured *center,* the Church, we must also recognize and fulfill the opposite view. We must admit the existence of the terrestrial element in the Church, through the presence of human liberty. This is equally necessary in order to understand fully the Church in the world. Ecclesiological cosmology respects the biblical tradition. It regards Christians as members of the Church, incorporated into the Body of Christ; recreated through and in her communion; sanctified and called in a certain sense out of this world, but remaining partly in the world and in full solidarity with it. As members of the Church, Christians are no longer of this world. They now possess a beginning of the new creation. Yet they live in the world and are recreated for the world. This is how

the scriptural words must be understood when they
affirm that we are not *of* this world, even though we
remain firmly and absolutely *in* this world.

Thus ecclesiological cosmology respects the absolute
primacy of the divine character given by grace to the
Church and acting in her by the Holy Spirit. This view
is still realistic insofar as the reciprocal exchange and
belonging of the Church and the world are concerned.
The Church is preserved from all triumphalism, in
spite of the glory symbolized in worship, presaging the
final victory of the Gospel in the world. Insistence on
divine priority prevents the Church from becoming simply another benevolent association made up of men of
good will. It preserves the Church from secularization
in the image of the modern world in order to demonstrate her solidarity with it. In fact, the aspect of "the
world in the Church" presented in ecclesiological cosmology is not merely a manifestation of the good will
of the Church, letting the world take its place in her.
Nor is it the result of an ecclesiological theology desirous of maintaining a balance between the Church
and the world. The dialectical nature of human liberty
motivates the presence of the world in the Church as
well as the opposition of these two. This in turn determines a judgment of the Holy Spirit, leading us to
consider the initial cause of this opposition: the demoniacal element in the world. Although, since Pentecost, this element no longer has the power to destroy
the Church, it is the element which leads all men, without exception, to turn aside from total communion
with God.

Without a demonology of history, in a theological
sense above all, rather than simply in a moral sense,
there is no ecclesiological cosmology. It would be impossible, without this, ever to understand the dialectical
reality of the relation and reciprocity between the

the Church and the world. The prince of this age, the principalities and powers who revolted, use their freedom to transform the victory of Christ into a life full of problems for the Church in the world. The salvific work of Christ accentuates the opposition of the Evil One. This work leads the sinful man to immediate access to grace, which has become through the Church the historical reality par excellence. The world is in the Church precisely because salvation has become through the Church an immediate, historical fact. The demon acts more directly in the near approaches to the Church, for his function is revealed by and in her.

It is for this reason that an ecclesiology which does not put the theme of the "world in the Church" in the context of a demonology runs the risk of falling into one of two dangers. Either it will be the prey of a unilaterally angelic, celestial triumphalism or it will fall under the burden of sin and see in the Church only the human, sinful element. It must be repeated unceasingly that the Church is the place, the means, and the event through whose salvific regenerative grace humanity finds itself transfigured and saved by God. It is through the Church that humanity at the same time repents continually, because man is under the oppression of the demoniacal element which is opposed in the historical dimension to this divine work. As member of the Church, man lives this regeneration, but he bears the marks of this lasting combat within the Church. He knows that his heritage is definitively anchored in salvation. As member of the Body of Christ which is the Church, the perpetual event of the transmission of the grace of *Christus victor*, man is certain that the world has been conquered. He knows also that he carries this world within himself because of the demoniacal element reflected in the Church. Thus the world appears in the Church not as a heavenly vision but under the most realistic and human aspect possible.

Why insist so strongly on this point? Only because it is necessary to stress the fact that the mutual indwelling, "Church-world," does not result from the social action of the Church, from a chosen or imposed secularization, or from her external identity with the modern world. This "belonging" is given as a supreme fact of God's trinitarian revelation. It is described in highly realistic terms in the biblical text as the outcome of salvation, which through the Church becomes an historical event. The various images of the Church in the Bible are the fruit of the experience of the Church in the world and of the world in the Church as an event situated at one and the same time at the center and at the extremities of history. The eschatological vision of the woman of the Apocalypse saved from the dragon which pursues her presupposes an historical reality. On the one hand, this reality is subject to the transcendental forces of divine action mystically present and victorious in history by the faith of the Church. On the other hand, this reality is under the oppression of the demoniacal forces which urge the world toward revolt against its center, its axis, and its own fulfillment. Thus the Church is not a human institution or an association of believers. Standing before the world or, better, with the world, she reveals her divine-human dimensions to us. She provides for us in a concrete manner the structure within which we are to experience the struggle with evil and the victory hidden in Christ.

On the basis of this ecclesiological cosmology the historical Church must always struggle not to give in to the temptation of theocracy. This would lead her to believe that all is even now subject to her divine authority and that she is prepared to answer with wisdom all human problems. The negative powers operative within the Church infinitely surpass the simple human phenomena which we see. They are more profoundly rooted in history than we in our holy zeal ever imagine. On the one hand, we must avoid an exaggerated optimism that would lead us to claim automatically that the presence of the Church is found in human progress, which consequently incarnates the Lordship of Christ. On the other hand, we must withhold ourselves just as carefully from all those enthusiastic movements which aspire to ecclesiastical perfection. Such movements seek to achieve the purity of the Church in a small community, emancipated from the Mother Churches. All these deviations are the result of a unilateralism and an extremism which have lost sight of the balance to be maintained between the Church in the world and the world in the Church. They seek facile, generalized solutions by placing too much confidence in humanity. Thus they overlook the historical reality of sin, reflected inevitably in the Church, which forbids us to seek refuge either in theocratic optimism or in puritan perfectionism.

Given this situation, the Church has no easy solutions to propose to the world. She cannot pronounce declarations of so universal a character that they are valid for all cases in all ages. Her *one* solution is to make of man in all situations a member of the Body of Christ and, as such, the immediate presence of the Church in the world. This is why Orthodoxy, while stressing the holiness of the Church, exercises her ministry in the order of morality and social ethics with an understanding of man which constantly takes into account his weakness and frailty. It is in this sense that her application of the *oikonomia* (*dispensatio*) of the law in a pastoral spirit must be understood.

IV

CHRISTIAN ANTHROPOLOGY

ACCORDING to the ecclesiological cosmology presented above, the theme of "the Church and the world" cannot be approached without a study of the subject of Christian anthropology, and this for two reasons. In the first place, the Church as an assembly of men regenerated by the Holy Spirit cannot be, compared to other associations or groups of men whose work, though excellent, is founded on humanitarian principles alone. Secondly, the ecclesiological schema just presented is important precisely because of the new man in Christ who, as a member of the community of the Church, acquires a new vision of this world.

We must, then, behold the Church and the world in the persons who incarnate and form every society and who constitute the people of God. Social ethics are not possible without personal ethics. From the Christian's point of view, priority must be accorded the latter. There is no general, global comparison of two great entities—Church and world—at the heart of our theme. Following ecclesiological cosmology and the vision of the Church as microcosm, through the work of the Paraclete, the essential point is discovered. This consists in the growth of man from his individual human condition to that of a person in Christ, a member of the ecclesial community. This growth implies for man a new mode of existence in the world. It is man insofar as he is person, that is "man-in-relation," who incarnates the bond between the Church and this world. The study of Christian anthropology preserves our theme from abstractions and generalizations.

Christian theology increasingly tends to neglect Christian anthropology, out of fear of moralizing. Theologians prefer to begin by a phenomenological analysis of today's world in order to determine the causes of its liberation from traditional structures and principles of morality now considered outmoded. Under the influence of pluralistic societies, every stable, universally valid principle tends to disappear. Man belongs to highly differentiated social groups which oblige him to consider himself a functional being, defined solely in terms of his social and economic milieus. Man as a unique person disappears. Instead of studying him as the foundation which gives essence and form to society, we now do the reverse. From society and its new structures the move is made to a new anthropology. The Church too is reduced to a depersonalized society, required to conform to the norms of modern society if she would maintain a relation with the world.

At this point, some confusion must be dissipated. It is absolutely legitimate to want to know the world and contemporary reality so as to be able to create new methods of evangelization; serious sociological analysis is indispensable in this regard. However, such an effort in no way constitutes the entirety of a study of the Church and the world. It is but one segment, to be accepted after study of the most profound relation between Church and world, namely, the action of God in the world through the Church and the transformation of man in Christ.

The problem today is one of knowing if those who speak about "the Church and the world" admit or deny that the Christian as a member of the Church is endowed by virtue of his faith in Christ with certain new characteristics by which he is capable of a distinct existence. The question is whether they admit that this man has not been formed only by the functional principles imposed by society. Does society shape man and through him reshape the structures of the Church? Or is man-in-Christ graced by his membership in the Body of Christ with a strong foundation which resists the simple, collective functionalism of society? As members of the universal Church, of the microcosm of all creation, of the family of men embracing all races and bridging all ages, can we accept the declaration that man-in-Christ is merely the subject of sociological phenomenology?

There must be no claim here to a Christian ontology of man which is opposed to the functionalism of modern society. There must be no pretense that social phenomenological anthropology is false. Christians, viewing man dynamically as the image of a personal, trinitarian God, find it possible to admit that existence precedes essence. But this existence is anchored and rooted in Christ. Far from the moral legalism of an anthropological ontology, Christians through the Bible find at every instant in the life of the ecclesial, charismatic community a new beginning. This in no way denies social development and its influence on the formation of contemporary man, today as in the past. Man-in-Christ does not possess a new human essence different from that of man-in-the-world. He has, however, a new existence, the result of his faith-decision in the Christian community. He becomes a new *oikodomè*, a new "house," whose solid foundation is the whole

Church throughout all centuries. This house, as *oikodomè*, must be continually built up on the same foundation by the Spirit, so as to become the abode of divine grace. Here, Christians have a distinctive basis for an anthropology that reaches beyond the structures and categories of society.

The exaggerations of one type of present Christian sociology and the absolute character of its positions run the risk of making us forget what is important for the theme under consideration: *man-in-Christ*. Man is regarded by certain sociologists as a cog in a social mechanism which dictates his existence, his aspirations, and the path he is to follow. In no case can the Church accept this sociological anthropology which gives no attention whatsoever to the unique value of the person in Christ. The mechanical concept of societies is one of the causes of the new theology and its generalized Christology. Without taking into consideration the element of personal faith, this mentality affirms the presence of Christ in the world wherever he acts through the forms of human community, bringing about perfect hominization. According to this position, the Church has nothing to do but decipher the marks of this presence, as so many signs of the times given by God. Even if this generalized, vague affirmation is not worthy to be taken seriously from a theological point of view, it demonstrates that all spiritual disciplines today have a tendency to take their direction from technology. Priority is given to universal forms and structures. Man as a unique creature takes second place and Christ becomes incognito in mankind's collective progress.

If we would grasp the importance of Christian anthropology as perceived through the life-giving work of the Holy Spirit and the ecclesial community, it is of prime importance to recognize that modern theology affirms the presence of Christ in the world without the scriptural postulate of personal knowledge of Christ on

the part of the believer. It is more or less simple, in a
way, to affirm the presence of Christ or even to pro-
fess belief in him. But the *knowledge* of Christ and the
acceptance of him as Lord through the Spirit is quite
another thing, much more difficult to attain. In fact,
knowledge here signifies to be born anew in him into
this world and to remain in permanent, personal communion with him, in spite of all social structures and
human conditions. This is not the simple knowledge of
an object—scientific or logical gnosis; it is the biblical
épignosis, which is at the heart of Christian existence.
This knowledge permits man, as a person first "known"
by a personal God, to know himself in depth as a member of the community of God. Through this community,
he recognizes himself in the world according to a new
perspective which is able to renew structures and to
behold all things freshly. Recognition of the Lordship
of Christ is the result of the primary faith-decision. This
faith must lead the believer to knowledge of Christ,
for he who knows Christ is in communion with Christ.
In and through the moment of this knowledge, which
results from personal communion with Christ, the believer and, by means of him, the entire world becomes
a new creation (2 Cor. 5:16-17).

This new creation is precisely not only that of the
individual person, but of the person as a member of a
creation renewed for him through personal conversion
in Christ. The event of becoming a "man in Christ" is
personal, since it requires a faith-decision, yet it is also
a community event. It is possible, that is, only in the
community of faith, and by reason of insertion into the
community-microcosm it becomes a cosmic, universal
event. All creation is renewed because of the man who
believes in Christ and who is incorporated into his community of believers.

It is for this reason that ecclesiological anthropology

precedes social ethics in the Orthodox tradition. This priority is of a qualitative, functional order because the human person and the soul of man are vested with value in an absolute manner in the Bible (Mt. 10:26). It is so, furthermore, because a community problem can never be resolved apart from the persons who constitute the community and are thus in the process of "putting on" Christ. It can now be seen why and in what sense the Orthodox Church has always insisted on a personal and ecclesial ethic before any social one. It can be understood also why, on the basis of this personal ethic, there has been so strong an emphasis on the element of cosmic vision. It is this vision which has caused the Orthodox tradition to embrace the totality of human reality and to create what is best in the arts, literature, and national life in countries which have come into existence as nations through Eastern Christianity. It must be added that if the Orthodox Church has opted first of all for the vertical-personal relation over that of the horizontal-social, it has not been out of contempt for the latter. Rather, this was done to give to the social domain a more solid foundation in the Christ-event. This event is possible, clearly, only in the ecclesial community.

Such a position can help us to comprehend more fully the meaning of the *theosis* of man in the context of Christian anthropology and that of personal and social ethics. "Theosis" indicates the priority of the divine act in regard to the human. Patristic tradition agrees fully here with the spirit of the biblical text in pointing out that the humanity of Christ is assumed by the divine Logos so as to reveal the true man as the image of the eternal God. Thus the *imago Dei* is manifested as the result of intimate communion between God and man, providing for humanity the possibility of sharing in divine grace. This participation is possible from the moment when the God of love reveals himself in Christ as a person who unites himself with sinful human nature in order to purify it. Purification is accomplished because of the union of human nature with the nature of God in Christ.

The new life is divine love poured out into the whole creation through the communion of all men with the Body of Christ. In Scripture, the Paraclete realizes the incarnation of the Logos of God in Mary by making the eternal life of the Logos the communion of God's love among men. By virtue of the Cross, this communion of love is new life for humanity. It is poured out through the work of the Holy Spirit into the entire world and in each man from the day of Pentecost, the historical beginning of the realization of this divine-human communion in the world. Thus it can be concluded that *theosis* is participation in the new life of the Logos, which has become communion of love in the Spirit throughout the Church for each one separately, first of all, and then for the whole world. There is, then, no question of a "deification" of man but rather of a participation in the grace of the divine nature. The Orthodox tradition gives priority to a vertical movement instituted by a personal God revealing himself as love. There is no intent to foster an individualistic mystique denying the reality of the world. On the contrary, patristic tradition, taking this vertical movement as point of departure, points to an authentic cosmic perspective and a relationship with the world based on a community of men renewed "in Christ" in a personal manner.

The two movements thus become mutually interdependent. Without participation in divine grace within the Church it is impossible to apply the biblical principles of new life in the universe. Far from being effaced by the personal ethic of the man-in-Christ, social ethics becomes both the end and fulfillment of this ethic. Just as the love of God is manifested and proven in one's love for the neighbor, so the horizontal movement of social action is the sign of the Orthodox *theosis* in the sense described above. Thus theosis signifies above all restoration of the true image of God through the communion of man in Christ and by means of the community of love of the Paraclete. These conditions lead to the true hominization of all men in this world.

One essential point marks the difference between the Orthodox position and that of some contemporary theologians. This consists precisely in the fact that there can be no Christian sociology and social ethics, there can be no talk of hominization by virtue of the humanity of Christ, without insistence on one premise: the experience of the concrete person of the believer incorporated into Christ by the community of faith. The Christian personalist ethic precedes social ethics. The former neither replaces nor restricts the latter. It provides a firm foundation for social action and prevents the development of Christian social ethics as simply another sociology emancipated from any personal relation between God revealed and man renewed through this revelation.

In its pneumatological and ecclesiological foundation, Christian anthropology is indispensable today. The great imperatives of personal moral thought and action which flow from the mystery of divine revelation must be kept in mind. In fact, the fear of falling into moral conformism and casuistic ethics leads us today to reject the personal call of the Bible, a call addressed to every man who must be recreated, as person, in communion with Christ. Modern theology is faced by the moral relativism of societies which are materially and technically developed and which, in their prosperity, have great difficulty in understanding the need of being renewed by faith. The temptation is to replace the difficult personal message of the Gospel in the world by

Christian sociology. Modern theology often presents an optimistic, idealistic image of the world so as to find in it a place for the Gospel, which is held in contempt by modern man. Contemporary theology sometimes chooses to close its eyes to the real need of the world, no matter what its condition. This need consists in the personal communion of man with God and a transformation which implies a radical change of orientation in personal life in and for the world.

Today the divine, prophetic word, "living and more keen than any two-edged sword, penetrating to the point where the soul and the spirit are divided" (Heb. 4:12), the word which judges, separates, and divides only to unify, is transformed into a harmless message. Christianity today runs the risk of proclaiming an evangelical message which is facile, sweet, and spineless. It does so under pretext of affirming the solidarity of the Church with the progressive forms of the world and the Lordship of Christ over the digits and calculations of technical civilization. Pseudo-Christian humanism can become a narcotic against the dynamic presence of the Gospel. The world does not expect the Church simply to propose one more sociological system. The world stands in wait for the Good News proclaimed without any compromise or ambiguity.

Once again, it must be repeated, the attitude being proposed here in no way underestimates the importance of the social action of the Church. It does not imply indifference toward the problems of society today or mistrust in regard to economic and technological progress. It results from the primacy of the evangelical message, based on the divine personal act in Christ. This calls for the priority of personal ethics and preserves us from a false, simplistic, generalized identification of Christ with the world. It keeps us from looking with contempt on the ecclesial community, on the prophetic word, on sacramental communion. In her confrontation with the world, the Church manifests an attitude which is founded on the value of personal renewal in Christ. This does not lead in any way to a sterile conservatism or to an extreme severity ignorant of the social ills and the politico-economic problems experienced by humanity today. On the contrary, this attitude of the Church is preeminently human, since it is based on the personal relation of a communion of love with the God who is savior and renewer of all men in the world.

This attitude is one of fidelity without compromise to the unique message of the Gospel. It must be communicated to the world by the members of the ecclesial community in a pastoral spirit which expresses the diaconal service offered by Christ to God. It is this service which must characterize every manifestation of the social presence of the Church. In all social situations, she must proclaim the judgment of God with and in his reconciling love. She must be a reminder of the humanity of Christ for all men and in regard to all human problems, even while she safeguards the authority of the prophetic word in the evangelical message. This *diakonia* must avoid both paternalism and an easy wisdom too ready to resolve all problems. It must be exempt from all theocratic aspirations. The Church is present in the world. She assists the world by her poverty, her suffering, her living examples of sacrifice much more than by those generalized solutions and systems which tend to deny the necessity of an ecclesial personalism. The strength of the Gospel consists in making each of us a new creature. This statement is the necessary postulate of any authentic solidarity of the Church with the world and of every action or social provision of the Church in the world.

V

THE CHURCH
AND THE WORLD

A FEW fundamental principles from the Church's point of view will be presented here in order to indicate the way in which solidarity with the world can be maintained without at the same time sacrificing the primacy of the divine act within and through the Church. It must be admitted that the Orthodox thesis in this regard is inevitably characterized, again, by pneumatological and ecclesial considerations. This is the result of the cosmic vision of Orthodox ecclesiology, flowing from a trinitarian theology drawn from biblical revelation. Hopefully, this vision is also a reminder of the fact that through and in the Church the world has received a new beginning from the divine grace of the Holy Spirit. Henceforth she can address herself to the various difficult problems which are met at the boundary between the Church and the world.

In order to clarify still further the attitude of Orthodox theology on this point, it must be stated that solidarity between the Church and the world ought not to be sought first of all in a so-called natural revelation or in the principles of natural theology. This problem has greatly occupied thinkers in the West. It has been the cause of long debates and quarrels which Orthodox theology has never known, because of its pneumatological and ecclesiological premises. The Orthodox Church has never sought solidarity in the order of creation alone. Neither has she looked for it, in any unilateral manner, uniquely in the revelation of Christ, which would lead to a Christianity denying the horizontal movement of an immediate relation between the sacred and the profane, between the eternal and the temporal. The Orthodox tradition has always been most careful not to unify the world on the basis of a natural theology that precedes the theology of revelation. This tradition has always been watchful so as not to separate into two circles or kingdoms the natural order and the order of the word of the God who has revealed himself. Orthodoxy has no ideal solution to suggest. Such a solution cannot be found, if Orthodox theology is attentively studied. The Church has been created as an event with the world, to remain in the world by the grace of God upon whom the Church depends totally. She represents a new situation which alone can enable us to comprehend all of creation and every terrestrial situation. Because she is the instrument which envisions the new creation, the Church does not take her origin in the world.

It is for this reason that the problem which is presented to Western theology has never been a problem for the Orthodox patristic tradition. This problem is accentuated by the new theology, which asks if Christ and the Holy Spirit are not imprisoned within the limits of the Church by an excessively Church-centered theology. The position which has been thus far presented here claims no monopoly for the work of the Holy Spirit in the Church. The Orthodox tradition affirms precisely this: that the spiritual basis which permits a dynamic life in Christ is rooted in the firm conviction that there is nothing in this world which is not the gift of the Holy Spirit. Furthermore, it affirms that the end of human life is the acquisition of the gifts of the Holy Spirit which constitute all of creation. There is no question of imprisoning the Holy Spirit in the Church. The question is one of receiving in the renewed community the same gift of the divine Logos which was given by the Creator-Spirit in the beginning. Thus the reintegration of all men into the divine-human family is effected in a new perspective. In this light, several specific examples can now be considered, not for the purpose of providing definitive answers or solutions to the problems, but in order to indicate the orientation of the thought and action of the Orthodox Church. In this way, it will be possible to discover for each particular case the attitude which is faithful to revelation.

CHURCH AND STATE

We know that Orthodoxy is not a Church strictly enclosed within one confession but that this tradition strives to remain faithful to the catholic and apostolic Church. Because of this, there has never been a prescription of laws considered valid for all local Churches, determining their mode of activity in every situation, among all peoples, cultures, and social structures. The Church stays one and the same in a differentiated world. She is one on the basis of communion in the proclaimed word and in sacramental life. She maintains everywhere the same tradition of missionary activity and of liturgy. This Church which is one and universal, however, is at the same time a local Church, a specific community, facing diverse problems. Thus the Orthodox tradition is careful not to propose a theocratic, caesaro-papist system, or to separate the Church and the state in a manner considered appropriate for all ages.

At times, a *symphony* between Church and State is proposed as a system representative of Orthodox thought. This is an exaggerated notion, on the part of both Eastern and Western theologians. The former are overly enthusiastic for the Byzantine tradition; the latter err through excess of the critical spirit. Nevertheless, it is clear that the Byzantine *symphony* served for a time as the necessary means of bringing the Church out of the catacombs. It facilitated the education of the masses who had recently accepted the Christian faith. It fostered the missionary activity of the Church among peoples who had not achieved national unity. On the other hand, it is true that cosmic ecclesiology in general favors a close relationship of the Church with the state, of any type whatsoever. The Church attempts at all times to collaborate with the state in order to serve the nation—taking this word in the highest sense of the term—but not totalitarian nationalism. In fact, following the cosmic-personal ecclesiology outlined above, the Orthodox Church looks upon the state as upon citizens who are individual persons called by God to share his communion. Obviously, on these grounds, there is an immediate danger from abuse of power, especially on the part of the state. Naturally, it must be admitted that certain Byzantine emperors and some contemporary politicians try to use the Church for their own ends, to preserve national unity, or even to propagate political systems whether rightist or leftist.

At all times the Church has the responsibility in this *symphony* to proclaim the prophetic word, for there is no political situation which does not have need of the word of God. The Orthodox Church has demonstrated that the silence of the martyrs is not only necessary to oppose an excess of state power, it is of the very essence of the prophetic word. A local Church which has accepted the *symphony* relationship between the Church and state does not fear return to the catacombs. The symphony should not be a nonviolent, passive attitude existing between Church and state. It should, rather, be the point of departure for an immediate, dynamic participation in the total life of the nation, with all of its immanent, complex problems, which the Church shares openly and frankly, without compromising the prophetic word of the Bible. The *symphony* should be an expression of the good will of the Church as she faithfully proclaims the Word and seeks to reestablish spiritual communion through a judgment in charity. The Church knows that *symphony* does not suppress the duality of the world, which is created by God's love even as it is deceived in its own autonomy. In every nation, the state stands as one expression of this duality.

Now it can be more easily understood why the Orthodox tradition can assume diversified colorations within the structure of a local Church, according to the autocephalous and national (never nationalistic) Churches. This is more clearly evident in the historically Eastern countries. The same affinity with the nation (but not with its political stance) can be discerned in Western countries where Orthodoxy has penetrated in the course of this century. Purified from every nationalistic excess, the Orthodox Church strives ever to interpret the *symphony* through adaptation to the local language for purposes of preaching, while preserving the liturgy's fidelity and prophetic accent. She prays at all times for the authorities of the country in which she finds herself, taking up full responsibility in the new nation where her task will be accomplished through her character as local ecclesial communion. Her desire and intent are to encourage collaboration between state and Church by maintaining at one and the same time a distinction between the two and a social, political solidarity. The *symphony,* however, has no power to suggest any definitive relation between the Church and the state. Indeed, this is forbidden. There is no ideal system, on this earth committed to duality, whereby the Church can find the means of living happily ever after.

These reflections help us to see also why tradition has always hesitated to embrace the idea of a juridical center for the universal Church, by which the autonomous national Churches would be faced with the immediate danger of juridical dependence on a center external to their own country. Here, there is no intent to criticize the Roman position in this matter. If we consider the history of the Orthodox Church, however, we can perhaps discover in this danger one of the reasons for Eastern reaction against the universalistic, centralistic evolution of the Church of Rome. The Church must be inseparably united to her people, so as to assist them in their problems and to bring them her prophetic word in its exact meaning for their immediate milieu. The local Church must never run the risk of assuming the appearance of a sacred, universal state within the local, secular state. In the eyes of the Orthodox tradition, this situation could give rise to an opposition between Church and state and to a separation between the eternal and the temporal which could result only in radical anticlericalism. The Orthodox *symphony* must be seen in the perspective of the local independence of the Church. Thus, it can be concluded that the autocephalous character of the national Church is the necessary expression of the qualitative catholicity of the Church. The totality of the truth-in-Christ which embraces the entire world is given locally. It is the expression, as well, of the *symphony* which should characterize all the efforts on the part of the Church to maintain a point of contact with the civil authorities and to collaborate with them for the well-being of all citizens and of society in its entirety.

CHURCH AND FAMILY

Here again, the problem lies in the manner in which the foundation of the family as presented in the Bible is interpreted. Natural theology leans toward a classification of marriage under the creative act of God and its continuation. This position is correct, for marriage is a basic institution in the act of God who created man as couple, as two persons who mutually complement each other for the propagation of the human race on the earth. Once again, there is a question as to whether the vision of the Church allows us to consider marriage simply and primarily in terms of the order of creation. The danger here is in forgetting human weakness and the fact that this institution has been profoundly affected by the universal fall. As a divine institution of the first creation, marriage has suffered a distortion which has deformed its sacred character. But marriage was not only instituted in the first creation; it has been reconstituted in the new creation by revelation in Christ and through the faithful, themselves renewed as members of the new ecclesial community. The New Testament speaks to us of marriage as the image of the complete union between Christ and his Church, accomplished by the Spirit. Hence proceeds our knowledge of the sacramental character of total union between two persons. Now it can be understood why it is not good for man to be alone. God has not created individuals to be independent and solitary, but to share a double dependency: the dependency of two persons before God and that of two persons with each other. This divine-human triangle is made known only in the personal revelation of Christ through his communion with the

Church and through the communion of his members one with another.

From this position, which grants priority to the ecclesial reality over the order of creation, important conclusions can be drawn for the discussion in our day of some points of conjugal life. In the first place, the Church must refrain from all rigid legislation and especially from facile promulgation of immutable laws which claim to reflect the official position of the Church regarding every problem in every situation. This kind of canonical legislation tends to minimize the reality of the fall, of sin, and of the tragedy of man's relation with man; it also compromises the charismatic and pastoral ministry of the Church. The force of law must never be accorded to an ideal of perfection which, though it may respect the supreme end of biblical morality, loses sight of what the Bible has to say to us about man as sinner.

According to the Bible, marriage is indissoluble. This same Bible, however, authorizes the dissolution of marriage in the case of infidelity between the spouses. This exception is made because of man's sins, not by divine ordinance. It indicates to the Church the pathway to follow in her pastoral, human activity. The Bible is not a code which spells out for us in a list of fixed laws the causes for divorce. The life of the Church interprets the biblical seed in every concrete situation. This does not mean that ecclesiastical marriage can be freely repeated. However, even while the Church affirms a single marriage and a single union between a man and a woman, she can employ the dispensation of pastoral economy and celebrate another marriage when divorce has been granted for serious and valid reasons.

The Orthodox Church insists on the high value of marriage not only in the area of morality, but in that of theology and of ecclesiology also, since marriage as a sacramental act is of the greatest importance for the Church and for the world. The whole Orthodox ethic is founded on the purity of the relation between man and woman and on their sacred union. Yet, according to pastoral economy, the possibility of a second marriage is permitted and, in exceptional cases, even a third. Thus the Orthodox Church escapes both an absolutely inflexible legislation which refuses a second marriage as being contrary to the divine order of creation and the indifferent attitude which allows marriage to be repeated ad infinitum. There is no ideal solution on this point to afford a definitive resolution of the problem. As in every other instance of a relational problem between the Church and the world, the Church must not be forced into a unilateral solution. Neither extreme conservatism nor exaggerated liberalism fully expresses the biblical spirit and the experience of the Church's life in the world.

Resting on this ecclesiological position rather than on the natural and sacred order of creation, Orthodoxy draws still another conclusion in this matter. If natural theology claims that the unique end of the union between man and woman is the continuation of the human race, it places this union itself on a secondary plane and neglects to emphasize the primary plenitude of the union between Christ and the Church as it is reflected in the union of the two spouses. The revelation in Christ focuses on a single fundamental reality: the essence of divine life is love. The creation of the world and the life of man are nothing other than the result of this perfect love among the three persons of the Trinity. All love between two persons creates life. The creation of life is thus its fruit and not some previous law. We can thus state that when the conjugal life of a man and a woman is total and complete, the new life which issues from their love is the expression of true union. It cannot be said, however, that marriage is unworthy if it consists in nothing more than the union of the two persons. The Church teaches at all times that the child is a new life which flows from, stems from, and manifests itself because of the renewal of personal life in Christ. She hesitates to teach that procreation is the only, primary, and supreme end of marriage.

It is not necessary to reinforce the second position in order to safeguard the first. Rather, the second reality must be subordinated to the mode from which it results. That is why the Orthodox tradition refrains from granting an absolute primacy to procreation, even though this reality is looked upon as a mysterious and sacred event in conjugal life. Over and above this, the Orthodox Church has no desire to become party to public discussion of or to express a definitive opinion on the birth-control problem. That is a question reserved to the most intimate and secret life of every believer, to personal confession before God, and to one's confessor and spiritual director. Without any doubt, birth control presents many problems and as a practice it is the object of noteworthy criticism on the part of the Church. Such criticisms, however, cannot be made in a general, public manner, out of ignorance of the limitations of the human condition and of the multiple problems which face the spouses.

The flexibility of the Orthodox position in regard to this thorny problem in no way indicates a weakness before the world. On the contrary, it admits the possibility of assisting the family which is an institution blessed by God, a basic sacrament of the life of the Church in the world and the backbone of human society. Furthermore, the family is that locus par excellence in the world where the love of a trinitarian God becomes incarnate in a visible, tangible way of life. The agape which unites the family is the apogee of all community life. The family is the voice of the Church in the world and family life is the para-ecclesial manifestation of the Church's communion. On this basis, the family can never become an object of superficial public discussion as far as its human function is concerned. Family problems are not to be subjected to extreme laws, whether conservative or liberal. In regard to family life, the Church must avoid binding its pastoral, charismatic activity either by negative commands or by the adoption of general theories. The postures taken before the world expose her automatically to severe criticism if she has recourse to automatic, general solutions while giving no heed to the specific nature of the problem presented in every instance.

CHURCH, SCIENCE, AND PROFESSIONAL LIFE

The problem of the relation between the Church and science today is relevant to the subject under consideration. This problem has become more acute since the extraordinary development of the sciences in the eighteenth century. In the West, this progress has been confounded from the beginning with the movement of scientific man's liberation from ecclesiastical authority. The problem is aggravated today, especially in highly developed countries. It carries in its train the emancipation no longer of scientists alone but of all the masses, for everyone shares in the gifts of progress and technology. No longer is the dialogue with a number of scientific minds, but with an irrepressible movement which challenges the spiritual authority of the Church on the grounds of a scientific vision of the world. Thus this emancipation is not simply the result of a progressive movement which denies traditional principles now looked upon as outmoded. It is the expression of the inability on the part of modern man, under the influence of positivistic science, to believe easily in his need for salvation through a unique, personal revelation of God.

The secularization of the European masses is more than a movement of independence in regard to medieval religious tradition. The most delicate aspect of this question for the Church today is that modern man no longer has easy access to transcendental reality. It is much more difficult to believe today than it was in the past. Besides, scientific research and the professional life consider as fundamental the autonomy of every effort toward greater progress in relation to any or every metaphysical and religious principle. Our age is still marked by the dialogue between science and theology which took place in the Middle Ages and the Renaissance. At the time, new scientific truths were proclaimed, threatening the traditional religious image of the world and of men. The supporters of these truths found themselves facing radical opposition on the part of the Church. Under such conditions, the faith-science dialogue stood on a most profound misunderstanding, and prejudice destroyed the possibility of any objective discussion.

The Orthodox Church did not have to concern herself very much with this situation, for Eastern countries did not experience the medieval and theocratic era known in the West. Furthermore, at the moment of the great development in the positive sciences, Orthodox countries were under Ottoman domination and thus were outside the pale of the Western world and its problems. Today, the problem has become universal. It presents itself everywhere with the same intensity and in all places it calls for a serious, deepened study. Even when the Orthodox attitude is not officially expressed in this matter, it can be discerned by a consideration of the ecclesiological principles described above. The Orthodox tradition tends not to conflict head-on with the general principles and postulates of science. In fact,

it is evident today that the Church should not be pre-
occupied with systems, doctrines, and general situations
which stand in opposition to a traditional Christian
attitude. According to Orthodox ecclesiology, it is of
prime importance to approach these difficult problems
on the level of personal relations.

The dialogue is not between the Church and science
or between the Church and an autonomous professional
life. It is between the Church and men who are scientists
or technologists. Now it is clear that there is no dogma
accepted today by any positive science as definitive.
Materialistic and evolutionary absolutism are outmoded.
We stand in the presence of simple propositions attempting to demonstrate their universality by experimentation,
by rational argumentation, or by some so-called universal law. Science no longer claims to take the place
of metaphysical faith. The sciences intend to, and must,
stay within the limits of immediate experience and so
contribute to the development of human life on this
earth. Once removed from political propagandizing,
contemporary science is ready to acknowledge its limitations and to work within the structure of strictly objective, immediate research.

When present-day positivism is not used by political
propaganda for non-scientific purposes, it is strictly a
method of work and not a creed aspiring to take the
place of faith in and personal knowledge of a God who
is dynamically present and active in history. The theory
of evolution is not aimed at destroying the notion of
man's creation by a personal God. Theology has spent
a great deal of effort in order to understand that the
exaggerated positions of some nineteenth-century biol-
ogists did not challenge the balanced, positive attitude
of the Church toward every new scientific theory.
Science can never be considered as an enemy of the
Christian faith, or even as a threat to it. If opposition

does exist between the two, it is on the basis of an illegitimate distinction made according to principles which are neither scientific nor authentically Christian. This opposition reflects on the part of the Church a concept of science which is founded on natural theology rather than on the ecclesial communion of persons called to be renewed by the gifts of grace of the Holy Spirit.

There is urgent need today for a theology of science. Such a theology ought to proclaim in an absolutely positive manner the unique value of scientific effort as a work given by God to man for the well-being of all, in view of an ecclesiological and cosmic vision of the world. This theology of science must no longer be concerned with scientific dogmas which seem at first sight to overthrow the traditional image which Christians have of this world. It must look to man in his concrete situation, called to become a member of the community of the Church and to develop the latent potentialities in creation placed at his disposition by God. In conjunction with men of science, this theology must undertake the study of the various kinds of human knowledge. In other words, it must provoke the basic question which no one can avoid, no matter to what degree he is influenced by any positivistic attitude. This theology must ask if there is not, alongside the objective, descriptive knowledge of pure logic, place for a personal knowledge whose limits cannot be determined by any scientific research.

At this point, cosmic ecclesiology brings us back once again to the scriptural tradition according to which the ultimate and deepest phase of knowledge is nothing other than relation and reciprocal communion between persons. The problem consists in determining if such knowledge is possible alongside other forms of knowledge. Certainly traditional metaphysics, such as it has been proposed by some theologians as the intellectual foundation of faith, becomes increasingly problematic for scientists. It would be ridiculous for the theology of the Church today to maintain the outmoded positions of rational metaphysics in the encounter with the world of science. She might rather employ the apophatic theology of Eastern patristic tradition, thus avoiding absurd and harmful dialogue.

In the light of the personal revelation in Christ and his presence through the Spirit in the entire ecclesial community, it is a crime to insist on theories which work out the incomprehensible mysteries of God. This knowledge is accessible only through personal communion with his body, not through reasoning founded on theories and on purely metaphysical and pseudo-scientific speculations. The vision of apophatic theology holds in respect the descent and the presence of God's personal communion in the world. On the basis of this historical event theology ought to lay aside all abstract dialogue with science. Theological investigation could then concern itself with the problem of the scientist's faith, a faith whose difficulties arise from epistemological principles rather than from a general emancipation from Christianity.

Finally, it can be said that the Church must be the first to renew and adapt her attitude and to recapture in all humility the original, cosmic vision of the world. In the light of this vision, one primary truth must be recognized in view of the revelation in Christ. This truth is that every man is called to the Christian faith and to the ecclesial community so as to become a co-worker with God the Creator for the development and fulfillment of all creation. This is the well-known Orthodox position of "synergy," which has caused so much misunderstanding in the West. For the Orthodox Christian, this is the crucial point which makes possible a new departure toward the just estimation of scientific work, as viewed through the man who achieves it. The Church must proclaim in an absolutely positive way the eminent place of science in God's creation. The Church reminds all men—scientists, professionals, workers—that everything they accomplish in the world flows from a charism, the gift of God, which is a talent they must develop by a personal offering to his glory.

In this way, men are enabled to become responsible for the fulfillment and realization of the divine creation. "Church—creation—new creation": a process to be put underway by the scientist and the technician. It is not a vision or an object of contemplation, but the beginning of a dynamic life of participation in the work of God and of perfecting ourselves and all mankind. The work of science then becomes one of the services (*diakonia*) of the Church in her cosmic mission, in spite of the catastrophes which are due not to science, but to human sin and to the demoniacal element resisting divine glory. The Church must remain faithful to her proclamation of the word as well as to the service which man—and especially scientific man—offers to his neighbor as a continual, living hymn to the personal, trinitarian God revealed in this world. In this perspective, on the foundation of their liturgical and doxological tradition, the Orthodox look upon scientists and technicians as sharing in the cosmic liturgy of all creation. Despite appearances to the contrary, it can be repeated with conviction, today more than ever, that the work of the scientist is a para-liturgical work. In the words of the Orthodox liturgy: he realizes in the world what is accomplished by the ecclesial community assembled about the eucharistic table. After the epiclesis of the Holy Spirit, this community pronounces the eucharistic word as its own to God: "What belongs to you, what comes from you, we offer to you entirely, for all, in all the ages."

The man of science and the laborer assume in their activity what God gave in potentiality in his creation. They make of it an offering for all and to all in God. This attitude grants to both science and the professional life their most profound and positive basis. It lays upon every scientist and worker an extraordinary responsibility, recognizing in them God's co-workers. Then it becomes clear that scientific endeavor and professional work become a reflection of the revealed divine glory. At the same time, this work is achieved in humility and continual repentance in Christ.

* * *

As epilogue to this brief essay on Church-world relations, it might be said that the Orthodox contribution in this domain will always rest on the primacy of the personal ecclesiological principle and on a cosmic vision of the world perceived through the Church. The foregoing reflections have attempted to show that this priority is demanded by the divine act which obliges us to advance in every circumstance by using the resources of man's spiritual life. Certainly, there has been no intention to deny the value of social action or of sociological analysis. On the contrary, this work is deepened in the Orthodox perspective, although it must proceed from a dynamic center which forbids the too-easy, generalized opposition of contradictory ideas. The dualism of the world as creation is at one and the same time maintained and elevated on the personal plane of faith in Christ and in his Church. On this basis, the Church can share in all problems, whether social, political, economic, or scientific. She brings to them an open, pastoral spirit, so as to aid man in his actual state as he pursues his daily work in this world. There is here no denial of the need of statements on the part of the Churches regarding the problems which afflict the world and cast it into the anguish of war, of moral corruption, or of social injustice. However, the most difficult work will always be that of personal contact, so as to lead man to deepen his own dynamic spirituality as a member of the ecclesial community, reaching into the entire world through this community.

It is our lot today to have discovered that "the Church in the world" is the subject which most loudly clamors to be considered and put into practice through ecumenical collaboration. Social pluralism as well as the unity of the world imposed by scientific development calls each of us to a universal responsibility which is difficult to exercise in a Church divided by sectarian tendencies. If she would act in the world as a primordial, regenerative energy, the Church must rediscover her cosmic, universal vision. She must keep before her eyes the totality of the world as one family united in the revealed glory of the trinitarian God. The Church can collaborate with humanistic efforts in the work of restoring the community of the world. She can share in every effort which strives to establish peace in the world, as well as in those which foster social justice and right relations among peoples. Many projects can be undertaken with nonbelieving humanists and with nonChristians, on condition that the distinction which results from personal revelation is never forgotten. This distinction is due to no superiority on the part of the Church in regard to the world, but to that reality to which she bears unique and permanent witness: the divine act of revelation.

PART THREE

Church of the World

P. A. LIÉGÉ

Introduction

For some time now, Christians of various confessions have discovered in today's world a challenge addressed to what they share in common at the heart of their separation: God's love for all men revealed in Jesus Christ to whom they bear witness. Out of this common bond are born undertakings of ecumenical cooperation concerning the great tasks to be accomplished for this world. These undertakings are still too few in number. The Decree on Ecumenism promulgated by Vatican II echoes the summons of the World Council of Churches in its recommendation for such forms of collaboration.

As Christians respond to the challenge addressed directly to their evangelical charity, however, it is quite conceivable that they will seek to go still further. It may be that their faith also will be stimulated to pursue a common search. It is scarcely possible for Christians to be in this world without asking questions. They live and act together, conscious of the presence of Jesus Christ and inspired by his Gospel. Together they confront a world whose visage is at times disfigured and bleeding, at other times radiant with enthusiasm. They find themselves asking: What significance does the world have in relation to Christian salvation? How can we express our membership in the community of men and in the Christian community? What meaning lies in the tasks men accomplish, in the values they struggle to realize in this world, in the light of what the Church has sought since Pentecost?

Without in any way abandoning the practical experiences of solidarity which they have begun to establish, Christians find themselves summoned to deepen their ecumenical dimension. This can only be done by means of theological reflection. There is a need to clarify the evangelical bases of their activity. There is a need to justify the kind of presence the Church must bring to a world in progress. There must be a more precise awareness of the twofold membership of Christians, taking as point of departure the exigencies of faith.

As soon as we set foot on this path, we perceive the work of ecumenism as response to an urgent need, internal to the Church of Jesus Christ. We realize also that the Church is summoned in this task to affirm herself and to reveal her innermost identity to the world and to its needs and challenges. Without proceeding immediately to define all the dogmatic problems which divide us, we can work toward the consideration of several of them, to the extent that each confession will make an effort to explicitate the way in which she understands and tries to live the Church-world relation. This is the aim of the present essay.

It is not easy to elaborate in a theological manner the scope of a title which seems to express all it has to say: The Church of Jesus Christ is also the Church of the world. This essay will consider four approaches to the question, each of them contributing to a development of the subject and all of them tending to converge. The first step will be based on vocabulary analysis. The meaning of "world" does not seem to be the same in all theological discourse. Many initial misunderstandings derive from this. The second step will consider the historical order. The history of the Church is necessarily implied in a reflection which would grasp the ecclesial reality after twenty centuries of experience. The third step will be founded on pastoral experience. How ought the dialogue of the Church with the world be presented? The last approach, more doctrinal in character, will lead, hopefully, to the beginning of a synthesis. All elements seen previously must be caught up and united in the light of several fundamental Christological and ecclesiological affirmations.

While rooted in the tradition of faith and supported by scriptural testimony, this research cannot be motivated by the hope of finding in Scripture some discourse which will be a panacea for all ecumenical ills. Still less can we expect to find a series of biblical texts in answer to questions which are at one and the same time ancient and new.[1]

[1] In an attempt to express here the Catholic positions, I do not deny that on one or another point other Catholics might well place another accent, somewhat different in perspective. In order to limit this inevitable diversity of views, I shall lean heavily on the final act of Vatican Council II, the Pastoral Constitution on the Church in the Modern World. For the first time in a Council, the Catholic Church has tried, with the help of non-Catholic observers, to express to all Christians and to all men of good will, what she is in the world and what the world is for her and for the Gospel. Without any doubt, this document is a text of greatest importance for ecumenical confrontation and cooperation.

I

"WORLD":
A COMPLEX CONCEPT

I T IS indeed remarkable that a great many recent
studies provoked by the conciliar theme of the Church
in the world include an attempt to clarify the vocabulary
employed.[2] This points to the fact that we are the heirs
of a language that comes to us laden with problematic
overtones. The Council discussions also bear witness
to this fact.

Before coming to the Christian meaning of the term
"world," it is necessary to consider the various connotations attributed to it by the human sciences. We
can speak of the world in a cosmic sense, to designate
the objective (or seemingly objective) reality of the

[2] Cf. Father Houtart, *L'Eglise et le monde,* Paris, 1964, pp.
12-18. J.Y. Jolif, "Le monde, Remarques sur la signification
du terms," *Lumière et Vie,* no. 73 (May-July, 1965), pp. 25-47.
C. Duquoc, "L'Eglise et le monde," *ibid.,* pp. 49-52, 61. B.-D.
Dupuy, "Une Eglise pour le monde," *Equipes enseignantes,*
2nd trimester, 1964-1965, pp. 73-82. Y. Congar, "Eglise et
monde," *Esprit,* Feb., 1965, pp. 344-345. G. Philips, "L'Eglise
dans le monde d'aujourd'hui," *Concilium,* 6 (June, 1965),
pp. 14-16.

universe, primarily in its material aspect, as the natural structure of human existence. This world is distinct from man and stands before him as an object of admiration, utility, or violence. We can speak of the world in an historical sense to refer to the total theater of human activity, with its persons, objects, institutional mediations, events, and situations. In this view, the history of the world is the history of humanity, embracing the cosmic meaning of the word. We can also speak of the world in a sociological sense. Here we designate one or another significant grouping of the facts of civilization at a given moment in history (the medieval world, the modern world), within some sociocultural space. Finally, we can speak of the world in an anthropological sense, as that global universe of human values recognized as describing the project and the image of man in collective adventure. Here, the stress is placed most explicitly on man and on the meaning which human liberty can give rise to in the unfolding of history. The physical universe, economic realities, technology, and institutions constitute the materials of a human world characterized by the building up and the promotion of man.

Is it necessary to underline the fact that this last understanding of the word is affirmed especially in modern times, in view of greater reflective historical consciousness and a more dynamic humanism? Thus the physical world, history insofar as it is an agglomeration of facts and accidents, and men in their reality as inhabitants of the universe are "the world" only because they are joined in a global project of success and accomplishment for man, by means of actively engaged human liberty. Earlier meanings attributed to the world are no more than the horizon on which the anthropological sense appears.

If we address ourselves now to Christian tradition,

we find again several notions attached to the term "world." There is, in the first place, the world as creation of God. Here "world" is the totality of reality, attributed to its author, bearing his intentionalities, revealing his power and his generosity. Man holds a unique place in this world. There is also the world perceived as vocational reality, called by God to salvation and an absolute destiny. This is human history, oriented toward the development of sacred history. "God did not send his Son into the world to condemn the world, but that the world might be saved by him," says John (3:16-17). The world can also be looked upon as the *dynamism of the powers arrayed against the Kingdom*. This world refuses to be possessed by the action of God. It refuses to recognize Jesus as the one through whom human history finds its absolute finalization (cf. Jn. 14-17). There is no question here of a totality organized alongside the world as seen in the two preceding meanings. This is a movement which is at work in God's creation in opposition to what it should become.

There is, again, the world in the *monastic and ascetical* meaning of the word. This world is the sum of the possibilities of complicity with the forces arrayed against the Kingdom, as daily existence in human society produces these forces. There is an understanding of the world as the *historical phase of God's design* in expectation of eternity—the present, actual world. "I tell you these things while I am with you in the world" (Jn. 17:13). This is the world of trial, of temporality. Finally, there is the world in the *ecclesio-centric sense,* embracing everything in human history which subsists globally in a situation exterior to the visible Church. This is not necessarily an exteriority of hostility and rejection. It is a phenomenon of stabilization at the level of human endeavor which does not (or not yet) coincide with the undertakings of the Church. In the discourse pronounced at Bethlehem on January 6, 1964, Paul VI declared: "By world we designate all those who look at Christianity from outside, as it were, whether they feel like strangers in regard to it or are so, in fact."[3]

The preceding reflections have by no means exhausted the full range of secular or Christian meanings attached to the term "world." Even so, it might well seem impossible to arrive at any precise knowledge of what is to be discussed in the attempt to situate world and Church in terms of relationship, one to the other. We have not yet reached an impasse, however. Perhaps the effort of contemporary theological language should consist in an acceptance and approval of the last-named secular meaning: the anthropological. In the consciousness of faith, we know what the Church is. We must then ask her to make herself known to the world, understood in this anthropological sense, before being prematurely ensnared by various Christian connotations, which run the risk of being too one-sided. This methodological hypothesis is suggested by the misunderstandings often caused in former theological reflections by an a priori definition of the world inherited from ecclesial memory. It is understood, of course, that what is authentic in the traditional Christian understanding of the world from ages when anthropological thought had not yet been developed will not be omitted from any serious considerations of the subject.

Starting thus, with an appropriate vocabulary, gives us the assurance of being at the point which is the world's consciousness of itself. The self-awareness of the Church should not be hindered by this, but augmented. Vatican II, in its Constitution on the Church in the Modern World, advises us: "The Council focuses

[3]*La Documentation catholique*, 1417 (Feb. 2, 1964), col. 180.

its attention on the world of men, the whole human family along with the sum of those realities in the midst of which that family lives. It gazes upon that world which is the theater of man's history, and carries the marks of his energies, his tragedies, and his triumphs."[4]

[4]*Gaudium et Spes*, 2. All quotations from the documents of Vatican Council II are from *The Documents of Vatican II*, Walter M. Abbott, S.J., General Editor. New York: Association Press—Herder and Herder, 1966.

II

A DIFFICULT COMPANIONSHIP

W E ARE the heirs of a language. More importantly, we also inherit a history of encounters between the Church and the world. Contemporary theological reflection cannot escape from this fact. A brief survey of the major steps in this history will help us discern the continuities in this area as well as the ruptures and the renewal to be introduced in view of greater fidelity.

THE FIRST CHRISTIAN CENTURIES

Paul, Apostle of Christian universality, gave this pastoral admonition to the faithful at Corinth: "Do not harness yourselves in an uneven team with unbelievers. Virtue is no companion for crime. Light and darkness have nothing in common. Christ is not the ally of Beliar, nor has a believer anything to share with an unbeliever" (2 Cor. 6:14-16).

In the light of Christianity's new perspective, the world was judged with severity. It was seen as dominated by false religiosity, as decadent in morals, marked by a dying humanism, and inimical to the heralds of the Gospel. It was, to be sure, a world to be evangelized. The mercy it inspired, however, was medical in nature.

Christians were to bend over the patient and cure him.
Nothing but contamination could be had from him.
Christians were a third race whose origins lay in Christ.
They were the soul of the world: "What the soul is in
the body, so are Christians in the world."[5]

Christians at that time were protected from a sectarian mentality and religious esotericism by their conviction that the Gospel was meant for all men and by
their hope for a conversion of humanity along with the
uplifting of the world by a new people. Their aim to
sanctify daily existence and the concerns of fraternal
charity saved them from retreat to a ghetto. The world
itself, however, when it was not idolatrous or distorted,
could be nothing more than a structure within which
the uniqueness of an entirely new world created by the
Christ-event was to unfold, in view of the age to come.[6]

It might be objected that more positive contacts with
the world and with philosophic culture soon took place,
as, for example, in the work of Justin. Even then, however, the perspective was apologetic. Some worldly
realities were to be used, but only to lead to a conversion without which there could be derived no value
from any of this world's treasures. In a word, the Church
was indeed in the world. She certainly loved the world.
But the world was temporary, perishable, and often
wicked. It existed only to be saved by the Gospel of
Christ. The idea never occurred to Christians that self-
subsistence might be accorded the world or that some
contribution might be made by them to its construction.

It can be easily understood why the Christian experience assumed this form in the beginning, if we take
into consideration the situation of the world and the

---

[5] *Letter to Diognetus* Chapter 6 (second century). This text
rendered by translator.
[6] Cf. R. C. Gérest, "Les premiers chrétiens face à leur
monde," *Lumière et Vie*, 73 (May-July, 1965), pp. 3-25.

intense, eschatological consciousness of the first Christians. What must be asked is whether such a position should last forever—even if that were historically possible. Should so minimal a dialogue and so pessimistic a view of the human adventure be maintained, aside from questions of conversion and entrance into the Church?

THE ERA OF CHRISTENDOM

There was never so complete an integration of Church and world that only a "Christian world" remained: *Res publica christiana*. The Church certainly encountered the world throughout the centuries. She inspired and controlled culture and art, social services, professional life, politics, leisure. She monopolized human activity to the point that nothing simply human had any right to existence, unless it had received the necessary Christian—or ecclesiastical—approval. The entire movement of the world developed in the shadow of the institutional Church, under her tutelage or in her service. Under such conditions, Christianity threatened to become an ideology, by reason of the claim of the Church to make authoritative pronouncements on all things. This extended to the level of concrete prescriptions about what man was to think and do and on the meaning he was to accord to his life in society. Christianity in this state was very close to being reduced to mere "religion." She increasingly excluded the free development of human existence from the domain of the profane and the secular so that it might be sacralized in ritual, in institutions, and in prohibitions.

It is true that these ages produced a flowering of civilization which is not to be minimized and a unity of the world which we have not ceased to regret. This was accomplished at the price of a confusion of tasks and a utilization of means which were humanly suspect.

There was such a limitation of human liberty, so great a spiritual imperialism, so poor a quality of evangelical existence that it could well have been feared that neither God nor man could recognize his part in the illusory harmony that was reached then. The Christian character of this world was too strongly imposed from without, too seldom the result of the free entrance of the human into the realm of the Gospel.[7]

In the domain of thought, there were many attempts at a more serious encounter with the world. Thomas Aquinas is one witness to this effort. The influence of his attempt seems to have been quite restricted, however. The development of monasticism, as far as can be judged, does not seem to have effected any equilibrium between the secularization of the Church and the clericalization of the world. Either this movement of monastic life was itself deeply imbedded in the prevalent system or its protestations remained merely ascetic and pietistic.

We can hardly recognize this epoch of Christianity as an ideal resolution of the problem of the Church-world relationship. On the surface, we can easily be impressed by the harmony established during the Christian ages, since at this distance the many contrived instances of that harmony are not always apparent. In the last analysis, it must be admitted that neither the

[7]Speaking of medieval Christianity, G. Le Bras affirms: "Masses of men remained in the grasp of the Church, subjects whose passive obedience, financial support, and fearful reverence upheld the authority, the wealth, and the prestige of the clergy. What inspired them? A faith which it is difficult to measure: at times fanatic, generally unenlightened, mixed with superstition and magic; a custom which had reached its millenary, and was upheld by periodic acts, such as weekly Mass, annual confession and communion, fixed and movable feasts; a juridical constraint more threatening than real which never acted except against heresy." (*Institutions ecclésiastiques de la chrétienté médievale,* Bloud et Gay, 1964, p. 589.)

Church nor the world was yet ready for a truly evangelical dialogue.

THE ORIGINS OF THE MODERN WORLD

The modern world has been fashioned out of successive layers deposited since the first tremblings of the earthquake at the end of the fifteenth century. This phenomenon presents itself to us, overall, as an immense vindication of mankind's autonomy against the world of Christianity. There was a twofold reproach made against this Christian world: (1) it had not sufficiently respected man and the value of the humanistic endeavor; (2) it had not, in spite of all appearances, lived the Gospel authentically.

Rupture with the world of Christianity was only one aspect of another trait of the modern world. Man was awakening to a new view of himself and of his relations with the universe, with society, with the realm of the religious. Geographical and cultural expansion, scientific progress, political and social revolutions: all of these elements were to constitute increasingly the horizon of a new universe of values. Universal concepts and ideologies were to crystallize this development and give birth to a collective conscience. Important elements for the latter were: liberty, progress, evolution, critical reason, independence, participation, secularization, free thought, consciousness, fraternity. A new optimism marked the terrestrial adventure of men. The Church seemed to have little place in this universal movement. An unfortunate misunderstanding was to develop between her and the world, during more than three centuries. We have not yet left this period behind us completely.

At first, the Church did not recognize the importance of what was happening. She continued to exercise control or attempted to exercise it, over the mode in which

Christianity was lived and over the elements of the new world—a world which disturbed her more and more by its lack of docility. The ideal image of man, which she had formerly fashioned to her likeness, grew fainter and fainter in the world. As the modern world gained in confidence and self-assurance, the Church took up the defense of a former world to which she had been more or less bound. To save face—and, she thought, faith as well—she warned Christians against new attitudes, she condemned new ideas, she retreated into the position of a cold war. She opposed scientific and philosophic rationalism, the ideas of the French Revolution, socialism, democracy, and the new liberties permitted in society. While she persisted in this opposition, the victorous modernity of the world affirmed itself without any reference to the Church.

There was misunderstanding here. The Church defended a status quo whose Christian identity was not as authentic as she presumed it to be. If the artisans of the new world protested strongly against an historical image of the Church, they did not always intend to reject the Gospel. Unbelief and atheism were not necessarily inevitable in this adventure. The man who was coming into existence on his own terms was not by that fact less open to the Gospel than the sociological Christian of traditional Christianity. In spite of this, it seemed that the lots had been drawn, the positions taken, and the enemies were irreconcilable. In its final proposition, the Syllabus of Errors, published in 1864, condemned Catholics who held that "the Roman Pontiff can and must accept and adapt to progress, liberalism, and modern civilization."[8]

[8]Archbishop Darboy of Paris is said to have written to Pope Pius IX on the day following the publication of the Syllabus and the encyclical *Quanta Cura*: "You have just pointed out and condemned the principal errors of our age. Turn your eyes now to what is honorable and good in our day and sup-

The consequences of all this for the Church are well known. As institution, she suffered a loss of historicity and of catholicity. Her message and her pastoral action lost in relevance. A ghetto mentality developed among the faithful, making them distrustful toward the contemporary world and constantly on the defensive.[9] Faith lessened in dynamism and became difficult to integrate into concrete existence. The life of the Church grew formalized and its creativity diminished. There developed an unfortunate series of alliances with everything in the world which represented conservatism and resistance in cultural, social, and political life. It was increasingly difficult to come to the assistance of believers who were tempted to break away from or relinquish altogether their personal witness. Christians who refused to establish themselves in the "purely spiritual" but who desired to adhere to their faith as well as to the world in which they were involved found themselves in an awkward position. Ecclesiastical conformity fostered suspicion regarding theological research, those who advocated reform, and those who were missionary pioneers. Pessimism flourished, some times almost defeatist in attitude, at the sight of the growing chasm between the efforts of Christianity and those of a "misguided," apparently irretrievably lost world. Praises were sung in honor of those regions which were untainted, existing precariously on the

port it in its generous efforts. . . . It is you who must reconcile reason with faith and liberty with authority." (Mgr. Foulon, *Histoire de Mgr. Darboy,* Paris, 1889, pp. 229-230.)

[9]Ozanam, in his judgment of the attitude of antimodernist Catholics, declared justly, "They do not intend to lead back unbelievers, but simply to arouse the passions of believers." Quoted by A. Dansette, *Histoire religieuse de la France contemporaine,* Flammarion 1948, I, p. 335. Ollé-Laprune, in turn, remarked that these individuals would have the Church pass "as the enemy of everything which interests the century." (*La vitalité chrétienne,* p. 57.)

fringe of the modern world. Naive judgments were pronounced against social phenomena (urbanization, industrialization, lay institutions, improved techniques of communication) and against those ideologies (socialism, communism, secularization) which were looked upon as responsible for the "apostasy" of the masses. On the other hand, privileges were readily granted to various forms of semi-religious and semi-political integralism.

There is no doubt but that the modern world developed the habit, at the time, of closing itself off to the Christian influence which might have come through encounter with the Church. It developed in pure secularity, finding for itself here and there ideological compensations and coming to terms with "religion" through a systematization of unbelief. Since the Church chose to underestimate the world and to retard its progress, the world came to lose all esteem for the Church, proclaiming the death of the God who had been kept by the Church from the historical movement then in progress.

These facts would seem to point to the conclusion that a death-blow had been dealt to the Church and her mission. Here and there, however, some few lights did appear. It was still possible for Christians haunted by the thought of the future of the Gospel in the world of their time to take hope.

THE PRESENT DAY

Pope John XXIII was led to convoke an ecumenical council by his desire to move beyond the tragedy of the situation described above, so that the Church might find once again a more authentic awareness of her nature and her proper role as a missionary Church in the world. The Bull of Convocation for the Second Vatican Council states this clearly: "While humanity stands at the turning-point of a new era, an immense task awaits the Church, as at every difficult period in human history. What is asked of her now is that she infuse the eternal, life-giving, divine energies of the Gospel into the veins of the modern world. . . . In conformity with the word of Our Lord, who exhorted us to recognize the signs of the times, we can distinguish in the darkness many indications which seem to announce better days for the Church and for all mankind."

Such a perspective obviously responded to the expectations of many Christians who for years had worked at their own risk to bring faith back through thought and action into the world in which they were actively engaged. It was not apologetic opportunism or apostolic pragmatism which inspired them. They were urged, rather, by the pressing intuition of a faith which knew itself ready for dialogue with the contemporary world. This faith had discerned secret alliances in the world, alliances which Christians had already discovered. In the world, their faith had encountered conditions of vitality and self-expression which they had not found in the Church. At the same time, this faith had recognized the dedication of those engaged in the human adventure underway in the world. These Christians began to feel most acutely the distortion in their relationship to the institutional Church. Why did the Church still hesitate to accompany her faithful in their encounter with the world?

At last, the Church in Council took the decision to overcome her timidity and acknowledge that Christians were right. She took it upon herself to reexamine her own situation and her positions in regard to the world. If the historical significance of Vatican II is truly recognized and if the intentions of the Council Fathers are concretely applied, Christianity will above all be liberated from her old nostalgias. In the opening address of the Council, John XXIII proclaimed:

In these modern times, many can see nothing but prevarication and ruin. They say that our era, in comparison with past eras, is getting worse, and they behave as though they had learned nothing from history, which is, none the less, the teacher of life. They behave as though at the time of former Councils everything was a full triumph for the Christian idea and life for proper religious liberty.

We feel we must disagree with those prophets of gloom, who are always forecasting disaster, as though the end of the world were at hand.

In the present order of things, Divine Providence is leading us to a new order of human relations which, by men's own efforts and even beyond their very expectations, are directed toward the fulfillment of God's superior and inscrutable designs. And everything, even human differences, leads to the greater good of the Church.[10]

Here again, there is a positive look at the modern world in its very modernity. The authentic concerns of man and the building up of a truly human community are recognized. There is no hesitancy about sharing man's optimism, even should this become tragedy. There is a desire to live with man, with no reproach cast against his pluralism or his secularity. The importance of the human endeavor is not judged with scepticism or jealousy. Christians are encouraged to take an active part in the universal human effort. "Therefore, by virtue of the gospel committed to her, the Church proclaims the rights of man. She acknowledges and greatly esteems the dynamic movements of today by which these rights are everywhere fostered. . . . The Church further recognizes that worthy elements are found in today's social movements. . . . This Council, therefore, looks with great respect upon all the true, good, and just elements found in the very wide variety of institutions which the human race has established for itself and constantly continues to estab-

[10] *La Documentation catholique*, Nov. 4, 1962.

lish. . . . This Council exhorts Christians, as citizens of two cities, to strive to discharge their earthly duties conscientiously and in response to the gospel Spirit" (*Gaudium et Spes*, 41, 42, 43).

Summing up this historical survey, we can say that the Church in the primitive Christian era scarcely valued the world at all. In the ages of Christian domination, she did so in an ambiguous way. At the beginning of the modern period, she underestimated and undervalued it. At the present time, she has declared that she is ready to admit its value without qualification. This final attitude has been called forth by the unlimited, unqualified character of the world itself which, from an anthropological point of view, has become more one. The consciousness of the Church has been deepened through an experience which has reawakened her original sense of historicity.

How, then, will the encounter take place, now that it is once again desired? Under what forms will this association be achieved? These are the questions that must now be considered.

III

CONDITIONS
FOR DIALOGUE

IT HAS sometimes been declared that, since dialogue is always effected between persons, it is not possible, strictly speaking, to talk about dialogue between the Church and the world. It must be well understood that the Church and the world encounter each other through the mediation of persons or communities in free and conscious activity. These persons, these communities share a reservoir of events and situations within which consciences from both communities strive to read the meanings essential to the dynamic action realized now in the world, now in the Church. There is, consequently, no reason why the Church-world encounter cannot be regarded as dialogue.

Albert Camus once wrote: "The world is in need of true dialogue. A state which is the contrary of dialogue is as much a lie as silence. There is no dialogue possible *except between people who are what they are and who speak the truth.*"[11] The dialogue of the Church

[11]A. Camus, *Actuelles,* I, p. 213.

with the world presupposes a certain factual otherness. We do not intend here to define this otherness in a doctrinal manner. It suffices merely to state that there is no question of the Church being "converted to the world," in the sense that she would confound her hope with the terrestrial hope of the world and struggle for its fulfillment, as she grows weary of waiting for an answer to come from above. In the measure that the world is truly world and the Church authentically Church, dialogue will succeed. The following pages will attempt to indicate some of the riches possible as a result of this dialogue once it can be authentically achieved.

LISTENING TO THE WORLD AND UNDERSTANDING IT

In a sense, the world is constituted outside of itself, by men and forces who have sought nothing else than to put man on his feet and to humanize reality. A priori, the Church's interest in this endeavor is one of sympathy and tenderness. This is not simply through protocol or courtesy, but because man is concerned here. The Church bears within herself the intention of a Creator who is imaged in man to the degree that he has become the artisan of history.

The effort to understand what man is about calls for constant openness. This is just as true in periods rich with hope as in times of uncertainty and questioning, as in the case of the world today. The Church will not arrive at this kind of understanding through analyzing the results of some inquiry or in being content with building a few bridges in the direction of a foreign world. She will come to understand the world in willing to be *in* this world and in living *with* it. "The Church . . . goes forward with humanity and experiences the same earthly lot which the world does." . . . "We must

therefore recognize and understand the world in which
we live, its expectations, its longings, and its often
dramatic characteristics" (*Gaudium et Spes,* 4, 40).

GIVING THANKS FOR THE WORLD

The Church knows that all things come from a God
who, in the Incarnation, has supremely recognized man.
She makes it possible for all that she discovers of the
human in the world, no matter how new or unusual its
form, to return toward its divine source. Thus she draws
into her activity of grace everything that tends to liberate
the constructive forces and energies of the world, so as
to multiply the possibilities of meaning for humanity.
She does not seek technology as such, material wealth,
accomplishments, in their raw, quantitative reality, but
in and through all of these she seeks everything that
affords new opportunities to foster human dignity.
Each time that a man receives such an opportunity, this
is a sign that the world is becoming more like what God
wills it to be. The Church celebrates these encounters
in the name of her Lord, each time that her presence
in the world witnesses to them.

COLLABORATING WITH THE WORLD

Those men who take the tasks of the world seriously
usually do not wait for the Church in their work for
humanity and in their efforts to bring this work to
fulfillment. The Church knows this. She is not bitter
about it. She knows, however, that in the name of Jesus
Christ she is an expert on humanity. She is able to unveil the true face of man and to promote its appearance
in her own community and beyond. When she offers her
collaboration to the world, it is not because she possesses
all the technological answers concerning the temporal
salvation of man. She does know in what direction these
answers are to be sought. This is the direction which

Jesus her Lord, eschatological Man, has confided to her.
The Council proclaimed this most clearly:

> This sacred Synod . . . offers to mankind the honest
> assistance of the Church in fostering that brotherhood
> of all men which corresponds to this destiny of theirs.
>
> All men, believers and unbelievers alike, ought to
> work for the rightful betterment of this world in which
> all alike live.
>
> The Church believes she can contribute greatly to-
> ward making the family of man and its history more
> human.
>
> The Church guards the heritage of God's Word and
> draws from it religious and moral principles, without
> always having at hand the solution to particular prob-
> lems. She desires thereby to add the light of revealed
> truth to mankind's store of experience, so that the path
> which humanity has taken in recent times will not be
> a dark one.
>
> Hence it is clear that men are not deterred by the
> Christian message from building up the world, or im-
> pelled to neglect the welfare of their fellows. They are,
> rather, more stringently bound to do these very things.
> (*Gaudium et Spes, passim.*)

CONDEMNING ALL THAT DISFIGURES MAN

Men have often recognized the absurdity and the de-
formations of the face of man in the world in which he
labors, without waiting for the Church to point out these
disfigurations. She does not regard this fact as one
which indicates some degree of rivalry. In her prophetic
consciousness, however, she perceives most sharply
everything in the realm of human endeavor which is not
conformable to the figure of a world true to the dynamic
intentions of God. She regards it as her duty to associate
herself in the combat against the idols of might, violence,
hatred, and injustice, with all men of good will:

> Furthermore, whatever is opposed to life itself, such
> as any type of murder, genocide, abortion, euthanasia,
> or willful self-destruction, whatever violates the integ-
> rity of the human person, such as mutilation, torments

inflicted on body or mind, attempts to coerce the will itself; whatever insults human dignity, such as sub-human living conditions, arbitrary imprisonment, deportation, slavery, prostitution, the selling of women and children; as well as disgraceful working conditions, where men are treated as mere tools for profit, rather than as free and responsible persons; all these things and others of their like are infamies indeed. They poison human society, but they do more harm to those who practice them than those who suffer from the injury. Moreover, they are a supreme dishonor to the Creator. (*Gaudium et Spes*, 27.)

Is this all the evil which the Church sees in the world? Certainly, not. There is evil in man's relation to God. If the Church can give proof of her participation in the temporal salvation of man, however, there is less danger that her prophetic denunciation of other errors and deviations, such as communism and the "sin of the world," for example, will be attributed to a rigid, pessimistic moralism. She assumes her position in the name of that prophetic mission which is hers, animated by an enlightened love of man. Pope Paul VI referred to this in a discourse of December 7, 1965: "The attitude of the Council has clearly and purposely been one of optimism. A current of affection and admiration has overflowed toward the modern human world. It is true that errors have been condemned, because charity as well as truth requires this. But there have been only respect and love for persons. In the place of depressing diagnoses, inspiring remedies, and somber warnings, words of confidence have gone forth from the Council toward the contemporary world. Its values have been respected and honored, its efforts sustained, its aspirations purified and blessed."

DISCERNING THE SIGNS OF THE TIMES

As she accompanies the men of her time, the Church becomes attentive to the language of certain events and situations which are decisive for the destiny of the

world. These are the events in which man's liberty is
particularly involved. They are filled with appeals for
transcendence and stand out in the course of history
in the making.

These emerging indications of human significance
are obligatory messages for a Church desiring to ac-
tualize the Christian mystery in her own community at
the same time as she would unveil the Gospel before
today's world. Wherever the signs of the times are
recognized, the future of the Kingdom is at stake. We
must keep close watch on everything in history which
concerns the manifestation of messianic times.[12]

The Church knows what she has received from the
world—from the modern world especially—for the
actuality of her life, her language, and her witness in
every case where she has accepted with magnanimity
and evangelical tact the signs of the times. Are not the
passion for Christian freedom and the concern for
religious liberty tributary to the aspirations for liberty
affirmed in modern consciousness? Is not Christian
universalism extended by the explosion of Western
civilization and the world's movement toward unity?
Do Christian fraternity and attention to the poor owe
nothing to the basic trends of socialism? Is not the
purification of Christian faith due to a democratization
of culture? Has not the deepening of the mystery of
the Church been fostered by the movement of secularization?[13]

The Council has understood things in this way.

The Church has always had the duty of scrutinizing
the signs of the times and of interpreting them in the
light of the gospel. Thus, in language intelligible to each

[12]Cf. M.-D. Chenu, "Les signes des temps," *Nouvelle Revue
Théologique*, Jan., 1965, pp. 29-39. J.P. Jossua, "Discerner
les signes des temps," *La Vie Spirituelle*, May, 1966, pp. 546-
569.
[13]Cf. P.-A. Liégé, "Quand le monde questionne l'Eglise,"
Lumière et Vie, 59 (August-October, 1962), pp. 57-73.

generation, she can respond to the perennial questions which men ask about this present life and the life to come, and about the relationship of the one to the other.

The People of God . . . labors to decipher authentic signs of God's presence and purpose in the happenings, needs, and desires in which this People has a part along with other men of our age.

The Church is firmly convinced that she can be abundantly and variously helped by the world in the matter of preparing the ground for the gospel. This help she gains from the talents and industry of individuals and from human society as a whole.

The Church herself knows how richly she has profited by the history and development of humanity. (*Gaudium et Spes, passim.*)

OPEN TO CHALLENGE BY THE WORLD

The Church has often been slow to recognize the signs of the times. She has sometimes turned a deaf ear to the world's message and thus has taken upon herself the responsibility for many misunderstandings. This is a legitimate complaint. It is precisely in dialogue with the world that she will come to recognize her passivity and to correct the misunderstandings. Dialogue is a school of humility. The Council admitted this. "The Church is very well aware that among her members, both clerical and lay, some have been unfaithful to the Spirit of God during the course of many centuries. In the present age, too, it does not escape the Church how great a distance lies between the message she offers and the human failings of those to whom the gospel is entrusted. . . . We cannot but deplore certain habits of mind, sometimes found too among Christians, which do not sufficiently attend to the rightful independence of science. The arguments and controversies which they spark lead many minds to conclude that faith and science are mutually opposed" (*Gaudium et Spes,* 43, 36). Regarding the question of atheism, the Council recognized that "believers can have more than a little to do with the birth of atheism" (*Gaudium et Spes,* 19).

As soon as the Church begins to dialogue with the world, the latter asks her, What have you done with the Gospel? What have you done with God? What have you done with man? The answer to these questions will permit her to explain herself and to justify a change of attitude as a return to the Gospel in view of the world's criticism and not as a mere tactic. The world, we must discover, is the place where the Church, often, verifies the Gospel.

CONVERSION TO JESUS CHRIST

When she sets out to live in companionship with the world and to realize a dialogue with it, the Church at no time conceals the fact that the look she brings to bear upon man is one with that of Jesus Christ. In company with men and in their midst, she shares the human project with all mankind. Bound to the Christ-event and caught up in it, she knows that she imparts a deeper meaning to every human endeavor. She is involved in a transcendent future, beyond that which is being built up in history. She shares solidarity with a divine enterprise. Even when she does not proclaim her ultimate origins, the Church cannot forget what came to pass when God inserted into history the absolute, universal significance of the Event of which she was born.

Hidden in communion with the humanity of God, how could she ever betray the human when she approaches it with her evangelical consciousness? This is why the Church does not hesitate to disturb the world at the same time as she accompanies it on its way. Does the world know that the solution of some of the problems blocking human endeavor, beginning with the uncertainty cast by death, is to be found in Jesus Christ? Is the world willing to admit what has always threatened and hindered the completion of its own building up and thus open itself to the call made to all men by Christ? Is the world disposed to recognize the decisive importance of God for its integral future, and to make a decision in consequence of this fact?

In her summons to evangelical conversion, the Church does not conceal the new orientation which she proposes to man, any more than she does the more dramatic character given to the human adventure by the entrance of God onto the scene. She knows, in all honesty, that she cannot be silent as she faces the world. She knows that, beyond all that is immediately perceptible, her call cannot fail to find an echo deep in the conscience of man. She can promise the world that what it has surrendered of its own self to Jesus Christ and confided to the Church will be taken seriously, treated with respect, and promoted to a higher service through involvement in a sincere, authentic hope. When the truly human finds itself in the Gospel, it no longer is homeless and a stranger, but can prepare for the celebration of encounter in a dimension never before suspected.

Only in the exchange of dialogue and in a language developed through such an exchange can the Church claim that "in her most benign Lord and Master can be found the key, the focal point, and the goal of all human history" and, "only in the mystery of the incarnate Word does the mystery of man take on light" (*Gaudium et Spes,* 10, 22). It must be repeated, for the benefit of those who fear that the call to conversion will destroy the attraction of encounter, that the Church cannot reduce herself to the state of a welfare society for humanity in order to favor dialogue. The honesty of dialogue demands that she state what she is. To fail to do so would be to refuse to go the limit in her love for men. At the moment when the Church makes her

testimony explicit and even goes so far as to affirm it
most specifically, she is not, by that fact, betraying the
world. She continues her exchange with the world on
the meaning of the human adventure, when she brings
it face to face with Jesus Christ. She extends her
dialogue in the search to understand the efforts of a
history that is in search of the absolute. She in no way
reduces the process of dialogue to a merely preliminary
pretext.[14]

If dialogue presupposes that each member be what
he is and speak the truth, this presupposition increases
in importance when dialogue is effectively realized. This
is true both for the Church and for the world, when
they actually live out the possibilities which encounter
promises. And now that this summary examination of the
situation has been made, it may be fruitful to seek out
a doctrinal systematization of what has been described
at the level of concrete, actual experience. As far as
possible, we will attempt to synthesize the results ob-
tained by the various approaches already used.

---

[14]In concluding his allocution to the United Nations on
October 6, 1965, Pope Paul VI referred to that ". . . unknown
God, of whom Saint Paul spoke to the Athenians in the Areo-
pagus, unknown by them although without realizing it they
sought him and he was close to them, as happens to many men
of our times. To us, in any case, and to all those who accept
the ineffable revelation which Christ has given us of him, he
is the living God, the Father of all men."

IV

THEOLOGICAL SUMMING UP

THE AVENUES of approach just examined, following the lines of vocabulary, Church history, and the experience of dialogue, have led to some useful conclusions. Henceforth, it will be as impossible to consider the Church-world relation in terms of dualism any more than in terms of some kind of reductionism. Dualism would distinguish the Church and the world as objects, leaving the necessity for establishing a bridge over the void between them. Through a process of reduction, the Church would absorb the world, dispensing it from having to live by its own energies; or the world would seek to absorb a secularized Church, appropriating its heritage.

Much is still to be done, however. At first glance, the needed effort seems to be in the realm of language, which must transcend its own limits in order to express a complex, dynamic reality. Even with the intention of avoiding dualism and reductionism, it is difficult not to give the impression of either.[15] Behind this difficulty

[15]This reproach has been made regarding the Constitution *Gaudium et Spes*. Cf. J. Cardonnel, "Le Schéma 13, une déception," *Frères du monde*, 37, 1965, pp. 105-112.

of expression, there seems to lie an inadequate doctrinal
justification. Perhaps this insufficiency can be compen-
sated for by a more systematic reflection on faith.
Earlier weaknesses can be eliminated and the limits of
language overcome. What remains to be done, at the
present time, is to become aware of the unity which
permits the following affirmations to be made:

*The Church and the world are included in a single,
unique divine plan.*

*The Church involves the world in transcendence and
thus manifests her uniqueness.*

*The Church exercises her mission only in historical
solidarity with the world.*

These three affirmations express jointly the dynamic
unity, the distinction, and the solidarity of the Church
and the world. This order seems appropriate for an
examination of the content of these affirmations.

CHURCH AND THE WORLD: A SINGLE, UNIQUE DIVINE PLAN

The statement above can be made, obviously, only in
Jesus Christ. In the mystery of Christ, the primordial
creative intention has been revealed. We confess God
as Father prior to God as Creator, in recognition of the
fact that in the creative act the first moment of a pater-
nal plan to be revealed totally in Jesus Christ was
willed even before the beginning of the world (cf. Eph.
1:3-15; 1 Peter 1:19-20). In the glory of the resurrection of Christ, God unveiled his creative intention
more decisively than he did in the story recounted by
Genesis. A direct relationship brings together the in-
tentionality of the beginnings, when man received from
God the command to ascend to the summit of creation,
and the day on which Jesus became eschatological man.
Without a doubt, the development of this relationship

passed through sin and the sacrifice of the Servant. We must take care not to underdramatize the work of the world's salvation. The recognition of the dialectical nature of the relationship in no way leads to a lessening of its strength and force. Rather, it enables us to admit that the fulfillment of humanity necessarily calls for still newer initiatives on the part of God. God himself ordained that this fulfillment took the form of an adventure, realized in history and through man's liberty. Finally, Jesus Christ was needed to take charge of the adventure.

Because God has absolutized the meaning of the human adventure and of man's fundamental experiences in Jesus Christ, we know henceforth with certainty what route it is that men have always traveled. Christian hope enables us to see beyond the present moment to that time when the totality of the human adventure will be realized in a way conformable to the ultimate intentions of God. This has already been accomplished in Jesus, who is the heart of the world, through an irreversible anticipation whose meaning is infinite and universal.

The theological categories which distinguish the natural from the supernatural order do not constitute a primary expression of the divine intentions. They are useful as an expression of what we have called above the new initiatives of God in the history of men. Too great a use of them, however, threatens to destroy the sense of a vocation to a unique fulfillment toward which God has not ceased to lead the world, whose source he is. The Sower has arisen with the dawn and the entire field of human reality has been sown. In this field, the Church, like Jesus, represents what has already appeared in witness to the divine quality of the seed and in prophecy of what the harvest is to be. Teilhard de Chardin was right to look upon the Church as "the portion of the world which is reflexively Christified."

The Church and the world must be situated in dynamic terms within the unique divine plan as two stages or two moments. The Church constitutes divine transcendence realized in the world so that it may become conformable to its vocation. In her, this unique vocation is to be made visible. This is the meaning intended by the term "sacrament" attributed to the Church in theological tradition: primordial sacrament (*ursakrament*), universal sacrament, sacrament of the recapitulation of salvation.[16] Even before creation passes into the eschatological Kingdom, the Church, when she is truly Church, anticipates in history the unity of the divine plan, through the phenomenon of emerging reality. In her, the figure of this world falls under the control of "the forces of the world to come" (Heb. 6:5), thus realizing itself as world.

Three "moments" that flow into one another permit faith to recognize that the world is the hope of the Church and the Church is the fulfillment of the world. These three moments are: the primordial unity of the divine plan; the ultimate unity of the eschatological Kingdom; the unity-of-becoming through partial anticipation in the Church of Jesus Christ. By *world,* must at least be understood the sum total of human endeavor which embraces creation and constitutes a meaningful whole in history. This is *world* in the meaning qualified above by anthropology.

TRANSCENDENCE AND UNIQUENESS

At the present moment in the divine plan, we find ourselves between primordial unity and ultimate unity, in a state where unity-in-becoming inevitably implies certain failures and a certain duality, even to distortion.

[16]Cf. *Lumen gentium* Chapter II, 9, and Otto Semmelroth, *L'Eglise, sacrament de la Rédemption,* Ed. S. Paul, Paris, 1962.

As we take this second moment into consideration, we must remember that we are situated within a movement created by the God of a unique plan. We can be thus assured that duality will never become dualism. We recognize that the Church is not merely the world and that the world does not equal the Church. There lies between the two a dialectical separation.

The Church was born at Pentecost of a summons from on high. The apostolic kerygma, which carried out this summons, proclaimed that the ultimate meaning of the world was to be found in the Christ-event. The fulfillment of all things found the source of its constructive energies in that event and there God became historically decisive in the human adventure. Those who accepted this absolute interpretation of what had come to pass in Jerusalem as real, became the Church, the humanity of the end-time, through conversion to the Gospel. The eschatological community became involved with the Lord Jesus in the ultimate process of the work of the world's salvation in and through the vicissitudes of man's history.

In becoming Church, the first believers did not leave one world to enter another. They brought into conversion their own participation in the world, so that Jesus Christ might be acknowledged as the center of this human reality. They surrendered the entire sphere of their existence to the Spirit, with their hierarchy of values, and their social obligations. They did this so that existence itself might be reinterpreted in the light of the paschal mystery and thus be introduced into the universe of ultimate meaning and into union with God. This engagement in the activity of Christ recognized as Lord of the world constituted the believers as Church. It is easy to understand that these believers, built up together by one divine call, could have brought into existence at the heart of the world a new community.

It had its own features, its own ways of expression, its means of communion with Jesus Christ. It was organized in a visible and social manner, thus constituting the external face of the Church.

What took place at the beginning continues to happen. The Church is composed of all human existence, of every area of human reality, whose meaning and profound direction are recognized as centered in and flowing from Jesus Christ, whose mystical presence is apprehended by faith. More than a mere formal superstructure, this Church expresses, makes explicit, and nourishes its being in a visible community in which the initial Event is actualized, celebrated, and diffused. The Church does not hide her uniqueness in relation to merely human communities or to those social organizations which she neither replaces nor dominates. Her uniqueness is not a matter of juxtaposition or face-to-face encounter, but of a rising emergence and internal dynamism which animates the human and widens its horizon without ever removing it from the world.

If it is true, as someone remarked recently, that "many believers no longer know what to make of this reality which is the Church,"[17] how has this come about? It would seem that such persons oppose the Church to Christian existence today because yesterday they reduced her to pietistic, ceremonial, institutional, and administrative aspects. The Church, in reality, cannot be identified in her sacramental and institutional being except in correlation with what is achieved by believing men who are a people. They are summoned unceasingly from the midst of the historical situations which they experience to be sent back into these same situations accompanied by their Lord.

Thus the Church born at Pentecost cannot remain

[17] E. Schillebeeckx, "L'Eglise et l'humanité," *Concilium* 1 (Jan., 1965), p. 58.

anonymous. She cannot be reduced to some spiritual
current working unnoticed in the world through the
building up of a human community. She cannot disguise
her frontiers, even while she keeps them open. She does
not hide the fact that communion with her Lord, the
Lord of history, governs her heart and that her pas-
sionately fostered attachment to him rules all that she
does. She does not conceal her desire to see as many
men as possible enter her community. She protests when
proposals are made to put her "religious" motivations
and occupations in parentheses, or when her witness
becomes embarrassing for others through her direct
appeal to God or to Jesus Christ. She protests as well
the accusation that she is not human, that she is a
stranger to the world—except in those cases where
she has to admit guilt in this realm. She does not need
to undertake a long pilgrimage in order to encounter
the world. She is made up of "living stones" (1 Peter
2:5) who are living, believing men. She has her roots
in the world in which men live. She sanctifies and
"christifies" the human reality which men experience.
It ought then to be expected that the true world would
find itself at home in the Church, familiarly at ease,
without undergoing any paralysis or distortion. It ought
to be so. If the situation is other than this, the Church
will not remedy the case by living anonymously in the
world.

   Another question presents itself, however, as soon
as the Church identifies herself clearly in the midst of
the world. Will this posture lead her to accept the fact
that there are areas in the world which are totally
exterior to her? Will this reality consecrate duality so
that everything not caught up by the Gospel in the
sacrament of the Church is to be declared non-Church?
This is a question that is most difficult to clarify; what
must be remembered is that the separation implied here

is only a dialectical separation, a tension within a unity of vocation. It is necessary, too, not to annex the world to the Church or to identify the world by this name without its proper consent.

What no Christian can fail to recognize is that in those parts of the world which choose to remain foreign to the Church, many characteristics resemble those of the world-become-Church. Many aspects of the building up of the world contribute to the constitution of an authentic fraternal community among men, seemingly like the project undertaken by Jesus Christ in the calling together of his Church. It may be an abuse of language to speak of an immense Church of anonymous Christians, in orbit around the nominal Christian Church, as has sometimes been done. Yet, knowing the unique plan of God manifested historically in the events of Easter and Pentecost, we should not hesitate to speak of types of the Church, of evangelical centers, of the hidden life of the Kingdom.[18] If these figures of the world cannot be called the Church, neither can they be qualified as non-Church. Furthermore, in more than one instance, a conversion to Jesus Christ has often been found to develop without any mediation of the visible Church and sometimes in spite of her.[19]

[18]"For, since Christ died for all men, and since the ultimate vocation of man is in fact one, and divine, we ought to believe that the Holy Spirit in a manner known only to God offers to every man the possibility of being associated with this paschal mystery." (*Gaudium et Spes,* 22.)

[19]J. Maritain expresses this in a most precise way: "It is not in the heights of theology, but in the depths of secular conscience and existence that Christianity acts thus. At times, it assumes heretical forms or even the appearance of revolution in which it seems to deny itself, as if the broken pieces of the key to Paradise, falling into the misery of our lives and joining with the metals of earth, could achieve more than the pure essence of celestial metal in directing the history of this world. The rights of man and of the citizen were not proclaimed in France by faithful believers in Catholic dogma, but by

The recognition of a dimension outside herself where those Christian energies which cause her to live are at work ought certainly to make the Church attentive to all that veils the Gospel through any lessened fidelity on her part. She must be humble in regard to the privileged service of the Kingdom which is confided to her. It would not, however, be normal for her to restrain her missionary zeal or betray the conviction expressed by the Council: "So it is that this messianic people, although it does not actually include all men, and may more than once look like a small flock, is nonetheless a lasting and sure seed of unity, hope, and salvation for the whole human race" (*Lumen Gentium,* 9). Mission often consists in channeling back to their unexplored source the subterranean but life-giving waters which irrigate the world. Some Christians might easily judge it useless to attempt to discover the source, being content with the admission of a distant, buried fecundity. The truth is that the missionary consciousness of the Church is more than ever aware of the tension to which Yves Congar refers: "How do we accept something from the world and still bring to it *something other*? How acknowledge what it already has and still open its eyes to what it has not? How help the world to see that it has a beginning of something which it does not want to admit? How does the Church preserve all its 'being apart from' without which its 'being-with'

rationalists. The last blow to slavery in America was given by the Puritans. Atheistic communists in Russia abolished the absolutism of private profit. This last achievement would have been less vitiated by the power of error and would have brought about fewer catastrophes if it had been led by Christians. The effort to liberate labor and man from the domination of money, however, proceeds from movements released upon the world by the preaching of the Gospel, as do those efforts to abolish slavery and to recognize the rights of the human person." (*Christianisme et démocratie,* Hartman, 1943, pp. 35-36.)

is ineffective and becomes nothing other than merely superficial association? If there were nothing left to bring to the world, there would no longer be mission! And yet, if there were no difference, distance, or separation from the world, there would be no mission, either."[20]

SOLIDARITY WITH THE WORLD

This final affirmation flows from the two preceding ones. If the Church is profoundly involved in a divine process of unity with the world and if she nevertheless establishes a movement of emergence which cannot be reduced to world, it must be admitted that her future is realized in a situation of historical solidarity with the world.

Solidarity is here qualified as *historical*. An explanation is necessary. Negatively, this means that it is not sufficient to state that Church and world can, from time to time, render each other some mutual service, when the occasion arises and when one or the other is so inclined. This would be nothing more than mutual use, each of the other. The Church has done this often enough throughout the course of her history. The world saw quite well that it was not being taken seriously and the Church, in spite of all immediate appearances, failed to draw the profit she expected from the operation. Some world leaders, for their part, have succumbed to the temptation to use the Church in an ideological and political manner. Many misunderstandings have resulted from this state of affairs.

Historical solidarity, understood positively, means that the Church knows that God has taken the chance of integrating his terrestrial and temporal advancement with man's history, just as he undertook the risk of the Incarnation. The Church cannot be herself unless she

[20]Y. Congar, "Eglise et Monde," *Esprit,* Feb., 1965, p. 358.

is willing to be bound to what man accomplishes in his collective adventure. This is neither chance nor determinism for a religion which claims to be the history of salvation; for a faith which has entered into the universal project of fulfilling the divine plan; or for a hope which involves the ultimate meaning of creation. It would be otherwise, if Christianity were a religion of idealistic salvation, an individual and purely interior mysticism or the mythical projection of human insecurity.

The solidarity envisaged here is interior, for it is operative at the level of man's destiny, where the meaning of the human adventure and his entire future are at stake. A common language must be the means of its expression. It must be active, for the Church does not give man to herself, she receives him from the world with his activity and his creativity. This solidarity must involve dialogue, for it necessarily is achieved through the liberty and the mediations of man's conscience. To the extent that a man of a given world assumes his historical consciousness with all his certainties, doubts, and limitless experiences, to that extent will this solidarity be felt and acted upon with urgency.

The Church should not refuse the trial imposed on her by this solidarity. It is a condition of life and mission for her. It is true that she bears within herself, and is aware of, the signs of the human made absolute, a condition realized by God in Jesus Christ. Yet she knows that signs cannot be communicated, cannot unleash their powers of life and efficacy, unless the world for which they are intended knows it is the object of their action. Christ the Lord remains "the same yesterday, today and forever" (Heb. 13:8). But it is in today's human endeavor that his lordship must become inscribed in transcendence. With conviction, in imitation of her God, and following the mission of her Lord, the

Church lives out a solidarity which is just as profoundly engraved in her historical being.

The reason just given as basis for the historical solidarity of the Church and the world gives rise to a question that is frequently asked and to which many answers are proposed: Is there an historical configuration of the world which would be ideal for the exercise of this solidarity; a configuration appropriate to the dialogue which the Church today must, because of her nature, achieve? We know how Christianity once answered this question. The Church cannot find a world fit to encounter it and historically open to the Christian message unless she herself provides this world by giving birth to it, fashioning it, enclosing it in her temporal institutions. In this way, the earthly city was deprived of its autonomy so as to provide a tailor-made world for a Church mistakenly identified with Christian society. The results of this notion have been examined above. Today, fortunately, such a position is impossible for the Church.

Care must be taken, of course, not to propose an opportunist theology adapted to the modern movement of secularization, as in former times a theology of the Christian state was invented. However, it does seem that several points can be made in this regard. Every pattern of the world which provides man with authentic opportunities of serious confrontation with himself, with other men, and with the universe, is one with which the Church can live. The Church would do well, then, to acknowledge this world for what it is and to assist it fraternally (not maternally) to be fully itself. She must not look for ways to stack the cards in her own favor. She must not pass judgment prematurely on a world which she does not know adequately. She must discover this world in its very process of being built up, a process which she must study. This position ob-

viously leaves room for successive types of civilization
and for highly divergent patterns of the world to emerge.
It does not seem possible to pronounce a value-judgment
more precise than this, or to express wholesale pref-
erences or exclusions on any other basis.

The Church ought not, then, find herself ill at ease
today in a world which proclaims its autonomy and
secularity, if she truly seeks to foster man's existence
and his historical potentialities. The mere fact that this
is *today's* world ought to arouse interest and friendship
on the part of the Church. In closer perspective, a forth-
right, positive secularity in human endeavor would seem
to be a guarantee for the Church. She will be increasingly challenged to renew her language and to make
relevant her message, instead of imposing, as it were,
ideally fixed forms. She will be protected against internal
worldliness and stagnation. She will be able henceforth
to act only out of her own inner life, integrating the
meaning of the Christ-event into the human meanings
promoted by man. She will have to awaken the world
to new horizons of faith with patience, taking as point
of departure what is within the world itself. Thus she
will avoid laziness and the illusion of a formal unanimity
achieved through purely institutional structures. She
will unceasingly reaffirm her uniqueness as Church.[21]

[21]Paul VI recently recognized this: "The Church . . . appears with a characteristic not always clearly emphasized in
past centuries. She shows her entire freedom and detachment
from all temporal interests. . . . Does this mean to say that
the Church will withdraw to the desert and abandon the world
to its own lot, happy or unhappy?

"On the contrary, she detaches herself from the interests of
this world in order the better to penetrate society, to be at the
service of the common good, to offer to all her assistance and
her means of salvation. She does this today in a manner which
differs in part from the attitude which marked certain pages
of her history." (Address to the Diplomatic Corps; *La Documentation catholique*, 1964, Feb. 6, 1966, col. 282.) (Trans.)
Cf. in the same vein, P. Ricoeur, "De la nation à l'humanité:
tâche des chrétiens," *Christianisme social*, Sept.-Dec., 1965.

Is this too optimistic a view of what the secular movement can bring to the Church? This depends, without any doubt, on the truly human quality of the fruits borne by it, for this is a movement threatened by grave ambiguity.[22] It also depends on the way in which the Church will integrate into this movement the Word which she bears. While recognizing the legitimate autonomy of terrestrial realities, Vatican II had the following reservation to make: "But if the expression, the independence of temporal affairs, is taken to mean that created things do not depend on God, and that man can use them without any reference to their Creator, anyone who acknowledges God will see how false such a meaning is."[23] This is certain. But does not the task of the Church consist in showing at the heart of human endeavor that God is living and historically meaningful? Does not the only efficacious refutation of humanistic atheism consist in annulling the challenge of the death of God by making him known as the source of those values which sum up the meaning of temporal man?

For this reason, we chose to say, with Christian Duquoc: "The verification of Christianity postulates what I shall call 'secularity.' By this term I mean the properly human value in every signification, for example, that of justice or human love, independently of any

---

[22]"That is not to say that the Church henceforth will be indifferent to error or that she is ignorant of the ambiguous values of the modern world. She knows all that these contain in terms of ambiguity, danger, and threat. But she more willingly concentrates on the positive aspects of these values, on what is precious in their content, on what is of worth for the building of a better, more just society." (Paul VI, cf. n. 21 above, *ibid.*)

[23]"If by the autonomy of earthly affairs we mean that created things and societies themselves enjoy their own laws and values which must be gradually deciphered, put to use, and regulated by men, then it is entirely right to demand that autonomy. Such is not merely required by modern man, but harmonizes also with the will of the Creator." (*Gaudium et Spes,* 36.)

ecclesial or confessional assumption. 'Religious confession' does not give value to the fight for justice; it
proclaims, rather, the possibility of ultimately transcend-
ing injustice. It is not the Church who gives value to
human love; she proclaims and signifies its eschatological dimension."[24] The Church proclaims and signifies
the eschatological dimension of love, for instance, when
she celebrates the sacrament of matrimony in the name
of Christ. In order to do this without falsehood or mys-
tification, she presumes that the spouses bring to their
decision, with a living faith, an experience of encounter
which has already discovered its human, personal, and
social meaning. She presumes that this is an encounter
where God has been at work from the beginning, in
view of making it holy in Christ. But the Church does
not create human love. She cannot even claim the
exclusive privilege of realizing the human conditions
which assure its dignity. For this reason, she is concerned about the pattern of a world where the meaning
of the man-woman encounter is asserted prior to the
Christian sacrament and even to faith in the Gospel.
So is it for all human experiences which posit conditions
under which the Church is to effect a Christian verification and the prophetic action which she receives from
the Spirit in virtue of the mission which is hers.

Perhaps still further precision is needed to remove any
ambiguity here. To recognize temporal man's greatest
possible advancement as the task proper to the world,
and to recognize prophetic judgment and Christian
verification as the specific work of the Church, is not to
espouse dualism. Only in the measure in which the
Church shares in the progress of man in the world,
through Christians, will she exercise her own mission.
There is no question of dividing tasks between two

[24]Ch. Duquoc, "L'Eglise et le Monde," *Lumière et Vie* 73
(May-July, 1965), p. 65.

parallel competencies, in such a way that the Church will appear on the scene only when the world has completed its work. The Church from the beginning has had to accompany the world, in expectation of the appropriate moment to intervene in its endeavor. She has had to cooperate in the human adventure, with all the artisans who are building the earth, for she knows the ultimate destiny and goal of their labors. What we affirm concerning Church-state relationships is not to be transposed as such into a discussion of the Church-world relation. In the former instance, the Church is referred to in terms of limited power and jurisdiction. The Church as the reality and mediation of Christian salvation is actively present even where she has no power to exercise, and even where Caesar legitimately wields his.

The solidarity which has just been described will become effective through lay Christians engaged in building up the world. Their status is inscribed in the very dynamism of this solidarity. As members of the people of God, they will be actively present within the secular city, working with other men to put it in the service of all mankind. They will be motivated by the intention of making the God of all men known there and of exercising their prophetic presence. For the Church, this means the actualization of the Word of God in the today of a history whose ultimate meaning is unveiled in Jesus Christ. It means that what occurs in the world is judged in terms of eschatological man. It means, finally, that the next step in human progress is always to be discerned in view of man's absolute future.

* * *

At the conclusion of this essay, we share the anxiety which Pope Paul VI expressed at the end of the Council, as well as the response he gave to this concern: "The Church has, so to speak, proclaimed herself the servant of humanity. . . . Has the thought of the Church in Council been turned aside by all that has been said, by all that could still be said, on the value of the Council, into the anthropocentric positions assumed by modern culture? No, the Church has not deviated, but she has turned toward man. He who considers attentively this preponderant interest brought by the Council to human and temporal values cannot deny that this concern was never disassociated from the most authentic religious preoccupations . . . by reason of the bond existing between human, temporal values and those which are properly speaking spiritual, religious and eternal. . . . The Catholic religion and human life thus reaffirm their deep alliance."[25]

Must we see in the conciliar reflection which we have chosen to echo and to which the Pope refers "the difficult confluence of the old current of Catholic naturalism and the totally new current of biblical and Christological thought"?[26] For our part, we do not subscribe to this interpretation. It is, however, precisely at this point that we must turn to the ecumenical confrontation.

[25]Discourse of Dec. 7, 1965. Trans. (Cf. *La Documentation catholique,* Jan. 2, 1966, col. 65.)

[26]G. Richard-Molard, *Réforme,* Dec. 18, 1965. Cf. what H. Roux wrote in *Le Monde* on Oct. 7, 1965: "In addressing the world, the Church ought not to be afraid to speak her own language, as long as this language truly expresses the Gospel. Formerly, she spoke of the first Adam and his metaphysical adventures in order to elaborate a disguised apologetic and thus justify the participation of Christians in the building of a world which had already perished. It is surely more human today to begin with Christ, the second Adam, whose obedience repaired the disobedience of the first Adam by engraving in his very flesh the one decisive act which is the basis of her hope and ultimately justifies an optimism which is not unconditional, but most concretely conditioned." (Trans.)

Notes on Authors

PHILIP MAURY is a French Protestant layman. Active for many years in the European Christian student movement and former Secretary-General of the World Federation of Christian Student Associations, he has been, since 1961, Director of the Department of Information for the World Council of Churches in Geneva. His writings include *Evangélisation et Politique* (Labor et Fides, Geneva, 1957), which has been translated into six languages.

NIKOS A. NISSIOTIS is a Greek Orthodox lay theologian who has studied at Athens, Zurich, Basel, and Louvain. He has held teaching positions at a number of universities and, since 1966, has been Director of the Ecumenical Institute of Bossey, Switzerland. Among his books are *The Problem of Faith in Kierkegaard and Contemporary Existentialists* and *Prolegomenon to a Theory of Theological Knowledge* (both in Greek). He is a frequent contributor to theological reviews and journals.

PIERRE-ANDRE LIEGE, OP, is a French Dominican who has studied at the Saulchoir in Paris and at Tubingen, and has taught at the Saulchoir, the Higher Institute of Pastoral Catechetics at Paris, and the Universities of Quebec and Montreal. He was a theological *peritus* at Vatican Council II, is co-editor of the review *Parole et Mission,* and has contributed to and written many books, including *Vivre en Chrétien* (Fayard), *Jeune homme, lève-toi* (Cerf), and *Catholicisme,* an encyclopedia.